Read, Play, and Learn!
Storybook Activities for Young Children

Module
12

This is one module of a total collection of eight. The following are the other seven modules included in Collection 2:

Module 9: *A Porcupine Named Fluffy*
Module 10: *First Flight*
Module 11: *Friends*
Module 13: *The Three Little Javelinas*
Module 14: *A Rainbow of Friends*
Module 15: *Franklin Has a Sleepover*
Module 16: *The Rainbow Fish*

In addition, there is a Collection 1 of **Read, Play, and Learn!** The following are the eight modules included:

Module 1: *The Kissing Hand*
Module 2: *Somebody and the Three Blairs*
Module 3: *Picking Apples & Pumpkins*
Module 4: *The Little Old Lady Who Was Not Afraid of Anything*
Module 5: *The Knight and the Dragon*
Module 6: *Abiyoyo*
Module 7: *Night Tree*
Module 8: *The Snowy Day*

Other products available in the TPBA *Play-Based* TPBC TPBI system include the following:

- *Teacher's Guide for Read, Play, and Learn! Storybook Activities for Young Children*
- *Transdisciplinary Play-Based Assessment: A Functional Approach to Working with Young Children, Revised Edition*
- *Transdisciplinary Play-Based Intervention: Guidelines for Developing Meaningful Curricula for Young Children*
- *And You Thought They Were Just Playing: Transdisciplinary Play-Based Assessment* (videotape)
- *Observing Kassandra: A Transdisciplinary Play-Based Assessment of a Child with Severe Disabilities* (videotape)

Look inside the back cover for ordering information.

·P·A·U·L·H·
BROOKES
PUBLISHING Cº

Baltimore · London · Toronto · Sydney

The Transdisciplinary Play-Based Curriculum from Toni Linder

Read, Play, and Learn!
Storybook Activities for Young Children

Module 12
Based on **The Three Billy Goats Gruff**

Module developed by
Myriam L. Baker

Michelle Gauthreaux

Richard E. Hire

Toni W. Linder

This module was field-tested and reviewed by Regina "Patsy" Boughan, Katie Greer, and Karen T. Harmon.

Paul H. Brookes Publishing Co.
Post Office Box 10624
Baltimore, Maryland 21285-0624

www.brookespublishing.com

Typeset by A.W. Bennett, Inc., Hartland, Vermont.
Manufactured in the United States of America by
Printing Corporation of America, Baltimore, Maryland.

Paul H. Brookes Publishing Co. thanks Harcourt Brace & Company for permission to base this module on *The Three Billy Goats Gruff*. Book cover from THE THREE BILLY GOATS GRUFF, retold and illustrated by Janet Stevens, copyright © 1987 by Janet Stevens, reproduced by permission of Harcourt Brace & Company. (See page 5 for bibliographical information.)

This curriculum contains activities and suggestions that should be used in the classroom or other settings *only* when children are receiving proper supervision. It is the teacher's or caregiver's responsibility to provide a safe, secure environment for all children and to know each child's individual circumstances (e.g., allergies to food or other substances, medical needs). The authors and publisher disclaim any liability arising directly or indirectly from the use of this book.

Every effort has been made to ascertain proper ownership of copyrighted materials and obtain permission for their use. Any omission is unintentional and will be corrected in future printings upon proper notification.

For information about Toni W. Linder, Ed.D., and the module developers, please refer to pages vii–viii of the *Teacher's Guide for Read, Play, and Learn! Storybook Activities for Young Children*.

1-55766-414-5

CONTENTS

HOW TO USE *READ, PLAY, AND LEARN!*

Think how much more motivated to read children would be if reading stories and using print materials enriched and enlivened their play. The booklet you are holding in your hands is one of several modules in **Read, Play, and Learn!,** a play-based curriculum designed not only to enhance emergent literacy skills but also to promote growth across all of the areas of development important for a young child.

The Curriculum

A storybook-based curriculum is not a new concept. Teachers and child care providers have, after all, been using books as an important piece of their programming for centuries. What is different about this curriculum is the integration of all areas of development into a full spectrum of activities, all relating to one book, with accompanying modifications and adaptations to meet the needs of *all* children in the class. **Read, Play, and Learn!** encourages children to *actively participate* in a *literacy-rich* environment of *playful* activities that foster *cognitive, language, social,* and *motor* development.

Module Format

Each module of **Read, Play, and Learn!,** using the magic of a different storybook, provides 2 weeks of engaging, theme-based activities to help children learn. This module, like all of the others, has the following sections:

1. *The Story:* A brief retelling or summary of the picture book, with information on where to get the book
2. *The Planning Sheets:* Charts for at-a-glance reference to all of the suggested activities to use for the 2 weeks
3. *Vocabulary:* A list of the key words and concepts, including labels, action words, and descriptors, to which the children can be introduced with this story
4. *Materials:* A list of the toys, playthings, equipment, supplies, food, and other items needed for the module
5. *Areas/Centers:* A description of 10 days of different activities for each area or center in the classroom, plus suggested modifications for the sensorimotor, functional, and symbolic levels of learning (described in the next section)
6. *How to Involve Families:* Recommendations to help keep family members or other caregivers informed, including sample letters to send home
7. *More Suggestions:* Alternative storybooks and other activities (e.g., songs, fingerplays, resources, software) that can be used with the module

In most instances, you will probably find there are more activities than you will use. This overplanning is intentional so that you can select activities that match the interests, abilities, and educational and developmental needs of the children you serve.

The Play Areas

The "centers," or areas of the classroom, include places for reading the story, dramatizing the story, and engaging in sensory and motor play; a literacy center; an art area; and sites for science and math activities, floor play, table play, outdoor fun, woodworking, and snacktime. The centers may be distinct or may serve multiple purposes. All centers may be set up in the room simultaneously, or you may choose to generate only a few of the areas at a time. Adding to or changing the centers for each of the modules to maintain children's high level of involvement is encouraged. For more background on structuring your classroom, refer to the *Teacher's Guide*.

The Teacher's Guide

Be sure to read the ***Read, Play, and Learn!*** *Teacher's Guide* before using any of the modules. (If you do not already have your copy, ordering information is included on page 74.) The *Teacher's Guide* describes the foundations of the curriculum, provides instruction in using the curriculum with children of different ages and ability levels, offers suggestions for classroom set-up, reviews the stages of literacy development, and helps you get family members or other caregivers involved. You will also find helpful information on weekly planning, team use of the modules, and sequencing of modules to correspond with holidays and seasons of the year.

The Children

Read, Play, and Learn! has been designed primarily for children between the ages of 3 and 6. You will find it effective, though, with children in your classroom whose developmental age ranges from 1 to 6 years old. As you progress through each module, you will find that levels of learning are discussed for the activities in each play area or center. By following the tips in these sections, you can adjust the suggested activities to the needs of the individual learners in your classroom. The *Teacher's Guide* and other products from Toni Linder (1993a, 1993b) will help you learn to identify the level of learning for which each child is ready.

1. *Sensorimotor:* At this earliest level of development, children are learning about concrete meanings through physical manipulation of the environment around them. They are more interested in the sounds of words being read, pictures in a book, and the concrete associations of the words that are meaningful to them. This stage roughly corresponds to the cognitive and language levels of children functioning from early infancy to about 18 months of age. This stage is also called the *exploratory* level.
2. *Functional:* At this second level, children are listening and watching, imitating, relating, and beginning to sequence ideas and actions. They are interested in listening to the story but are still more interested in talking about the pictures than telling the story per se. This level coincides approximately with children functioning from about 18 months to 3 years of age.
3. *Symbolic:* When children become interested in learning and representing their understanding through a variety of representational and symbolic

means, including fantasy play, storytelling, music, dance, art, drawing, and print, they have reached the symbolic level. Children at this level, typically 3 years of age or older, become interested in the print in the picture book, the story sequence, and the telling of the story.

Why Should I Use Read, Play, and Learn!?

The advantages of **Read, Play, and Learn!** are many. The use of the same storybook over 2 weeks (it can be extended to a longer period of time if desired) allows repeated encounters with themes and concepts and the modification, adaptation, and generalization of skills related to those ideas across time and from school to home. The reiteration of concepts and themes provides opportunities for understanding in multiple ways. The development of projects allows children to work at their own pace. Repeated exposure to activities builds memory skills. Actions, events, characters, language structures, and vocabulary are increasingly understood, retained, and applied. In short, each story, and its related activities, serves as the stimulus for discussion, play, exploration, investigation, dramatization, creative expression, socialization, and emerging literacy development.

Now, to Get Started . . .

You will first want to familiarize yourself with the content of the *Teacher's Guide* and several of the modules. Then, choose a sequence of modules that makes the most sense for the time of year you are starting to use the curriculum and the children with whom you are working.

Read through the complete module. If you do not already have a copy of the storybook, obtain one. Each story associated with a module is a popular children's book available in most bookstores and libraries, but if you are not able to find the exact book, at the back of the module you will find a list of other books that you can substitute.

Refer to the Planning Sheets to see how the storybook becomes the basis for each day's activities. Then, gather the materials you will need, and plan how you want to set up your classroom. Everything you will need is identified in the Materials section of the module.

Now you are ready to use the daily suggestions in the areas/centers of the module to make **Read, Play, and Learn!** work in your classroom or child care center. The *Teacher's Guide* will give you more information on the importance of starting each day with the reading of the story followed by an acting out or dramatization. Each day you will embellish the reading and involve the children more; ideas for how to do this across the 2 weeks are included in the module. Then you can choose from among the many descriptions of specific activities for each area or center you set up. You may follow the Planning Sheets exactly or you may use the Planning Sheet Master in the Appendix at the end of the *Teacher's Guide* to modify and adapt the storybook modules for the children in your classroom. Each of these sections of the module is followed by tips on how to modify the activities so that all children benefit whether they are sensorimotor, functional, or symbolic learners. You'll be able to teach or supervise children in groups but still individualize the instruction to suit each child.

The *Teacher's Guide* includes suggestions for adaptations and modifications to use the curriculum with children with disabilities or special needs. By using

Read, Play, and Learn! in conjunction with Toni Linder's other products, *Transdisciplinary Play-Based Assessment* and *Transdisciplinary Play-Based Intervention* (1993a, 1993b), you'll make your classroom an inclusive learning environment. (To order either of these books, with more information on individualized family service plans and individualized education programs, refer to page 74.)

Before you are actually under way, be sure to read the important section on involving families. You'll want to let the care providers of the children you see each day know which story is being discussed in school so that learning can extend to the home. By sending home a letter of explanation and perhaps even a modified version of the Planning Sheets for the story, parents can work on vocabulary, themes, and concepts at home. The more parents know about what is happening during the day, the more they will have to talk about with their children. Some families will even go to the library or bookstore to have a copy of the storybook at home.

Have Fun! So, turn your classroom into a place for dialogue, discourse, and discovery, not just question and response. Modify and create; inspire and stimulate. Have fun, and the children you teach or care for will, too!

References

Linder, T.W. (1993a). *Transdisciplinary play-based assessment: A functional approach to working with young children* (Rev. ed.). Baltimore: Paul H. Brookes Publishing Co.

Linder, T.W. (1993b). *Transdisciplinary play-based intervention: Guidelines for developing a meaningful curriculum for young children*. Baltimore: Paul H. Brookes Publishing Co.

THE STORY

The Three Billy Goats Gruff, retold and illustrated by Janet Stevens, is the familiar story of three brother goats who encounter a troll. The illustrations have been modernized with details that children will love. *The Three Billy Goats Gruff* is also a story about families sticking together and facing fear with courage. The three billy goats have run out of grass on their side of the valley and must cross a bridge to the other side. Under the bridge is a mean and scary troll, whom all three goats must face in order to cross the bridge. As the troll roars his challenge and threatens to eat each of the younger goats, they plead that their older brother is bigger and juicier than they are. This plea works for each of the younger two goats; when the eldest goat crosses, he meets the troll's challenge and "kicks, pokes, and scares" him away. The three billy goats are united on the far side of the bridge where they remain, eating sweet, green grass.

This story can be used to help children explore their own fears of things, real or imagined, as well as how other family members can help to cope with fear. For some children, family structure may be a more important issue to focus on. The story provides many opportunities to cope with separation from family, nontraditional family structure, and fear and courage in people of all ages.

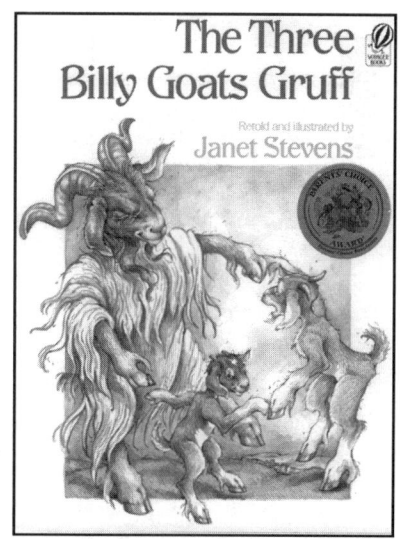

Title:	*The Three Billy Goats Gruff*
Retold and illustrated by:	Janet Stevens
Publisher:	Voyager Books
Price:	$6.00*

Winner of the Parents' Choice Award, Parents' Choice Foundation.

Try your local bookstore or library to obtain this book.
*Suggested retail price

Play-Based Curriculum Planning Sheet: Storybook Activities

Date: Week One   **Theme (optional):** Bravery/Family   **Book title (optional):** The Three Billy Goats Gruff

Play area	Monday	Tuesday	Wednesday	Thursday	Friday
Reading the Story	Read the story to the children. Talk about times when they have been afraid. Let them identify each of the characters.	Read the story to the children, showing them the pictures and allowing them to name the different characters as they appear.	Read the story again. Prompt the children to fill in the sounds that the goats make when crossing the bridge and the words that the troll says.	Read the story, and let the children fill in as many words as they can. Point to the words in the book as they are read.	Let the children "read" the story while you sign key words. Let the children take turns being characters.
Dramatic Play: Theme Area	Let the children play on and around the bridge, using the clothing to mimic the goats and the troll.	Facilitate the children's acting out the story. Model if necessary. Add the troll's pet frog.	Allow the children to act out the story with support as needed. Incorporate the troll masks made in the Art Area.	Have the children help make an obstacle course over and under the bridge and then act out the story. Begin to fade facilitation.	Incorporate into play the goat masks made in the Art Area. Set up a fishing game for the children.
Literacy Center	Write a letter home requesting pictures of the family. Make a larger "book" for the children.	Continue to have the story and big book available. Begin work on the Family Books. Have children dictate captions.	Continue to have the tape of the story and big book available. Continue to make Family Books. Add captions as needed.	Continue to have the tape of the story and big book available. Have the children discuss their "family shapes."	Continue to have the tape of the story and big book available. Take Polaroid pictures of each child's "special friend."
Science and Math Center	Begin working on a class grass garden and on individual gardens. Play matching games with colors, shapes, and numbers.	Make number puzzles. Play the Foods that Animals Eat matching game. Repeat the matching games.	Bring a tadpole to class. Discuss with the children how it will grow into a frog. Have pictures showing each stage of growth. Observe the grass gardens.	Continue to play Foods that Animals Eat. Play the Smallest to Biggest game. Continue to observe the gardens.	Play Fishing Bingo. Begin working on creating an animal homes scene. Continue to observe the gardens.
Art Area	Create troll masks from cardboard or paper plates. Decorate them for use in the Dramatic Play: Theme Area.	Make goat masks for use in the Dramatic Play: Theme Area. Finish making the troll masks. Create and decorate the troll's cave.	Let the children draw or design goats or trolls. Continue making goat masks.	Make three-dimensional goats from paper towel or toilet paper tubes. Discuss the body parts and characteristics of goats as you make them.	Continue making three-dimensional goats. Create nature collages.
Sensory Area	Make stretchy green grass using a picture chart. Let it sit overnight.	Let the children experiment with the stretchy green grass. Have the children explore different ways to make the "trip-trap" sound.	Create a texture game. Make a grid, and in each square glue an item with a different texture. Have the children describe the items.	Continue playing in the exploration area. Repeat the texture game, or turn it into a texture relay.	Continue playing in the exploration area and with the textures. Explore the skin, hooves, horns, skulls, leather, and so forth of different animals.
Motor Area	Create a scene that is similar to that in the story. As the children act out the story, they will need to maneuver up and over the bridge and down into the meadow.	Practice some of the motor skills that occur in the story. Discuss how far different things can run, jump, and so forth.	A low balance beam can become the bridge. Place a mat on the floor next to the "bridge," and let the children pretend to fall off and roll onto the mat.	Make human bridges and tunnels. Have some of the children be the billy goats and go over and through the bridges and tunnels.	Make a body obstacle course. Have the children be the billy goats and go over, under, between, and around different obstacles.

From Read, Play, and Learn! by Toni W. Linder © 1999 by Paul H. Brookes Publishing Co., Inc.

TPBA   Play-Based   TPBI
TPBC

Play-Based Curriculum Planning Sheet: Storybook Activities

Date: Week One   **Theme (optional):** Bravery/Family   **Book title (optional):** The Three Billy Goats Gruff

Play area	Monday	Tuesday	Wednesday	Thursday	Friday
Floor Play	Begin creating a miniature scenario. Have puzzles available that include frogs and other outdoor animals.	Continue to play with and add to the miniature scenario. Add plastic animals. Have puzzles available. Play Go Fish!	Continue playing with and adding to the scenario. Add nature materials to the scene. Play Baby Animal Lotto.	Continue playing with and adding to the scenario. Add small signs for the bridge, meadow, barn, troll, cave, and so forth.	Continue playing with and adding to the scenario. Let the children modify the scene. Do the Farm Friends Giant Floor Puzzle.
Table Play	Begin work on creating a puppet stage. Let the children decorate the stage curtain.	Continue to work on puppet stage. Make billy goats and a troll walking puppets. Stage a puppet show.	Continue working on the puppet stage. Add nature materials to the scene. Continue making the walking puppets.	Create a nature scene for their puppets. Continue puppet stage play. Make fishing game.	Let the children make magnetic goats, bridges, trees, and trolls for the magnetic board. Continue puppet stage play.
Outdoor Play	Play Troll Hide-and-Seek. Free play.	Use cardboard boxes for caves. Trip-trap with soft and loud steps. Play Troll Hide-and-Seek. Free play.	Have a scavenger hunt for objects outside. Free Play.	Draw a mean troll face on a ball. Let the children stand in a circle around the ball. The point of the game is to keep the ball moving. Free play.	Create an outdoor dramatic area to reenact the story. Make tin-can stilts. Free play.
Snack	Oral motor: Teach the children to flick their tongues like frogs. Do the Three Frogs fingerplay. Snack: Goat salad and carrot juice	Oral motor: Repeat the tongue activity. Sing "Are You Listening?" Snack: Bread with butter or peanut butter and milk	Oral motor: Pretend to be trolls gnashing teeth. Snack: Carrot sticks, pepper sticks, and celery sticks and veggie juice	Oral motor: Experiment with troll noises. Do the Three Little Billy Goats fingerplay. Snack: Troll's nose on a bun with milk	Oral motor: Repeat troll noises and faces. Snack: Crackers with cream cheese and alfalfa sprouts and water
Books and Music					
Software					

From *Read, Play, and Learn!* by Toni W. Linder © 1999 by Paul H. Brookes Publishing Co., Inc.

TPBA *Play-Based* TPBC

Play-Based TPBI

Play-Based Curriculum Planning Sheet: Storybook Activities

Date: _Week Two_   **Theme (optional):** _Bravery/Family_   **Book title (optional):** _The Three Billy Goats Gruff_

Play area	Monday	Tuesday	Wednesday	Thursday	Friday
Reading the Story	Let the children tell the story and act out the parts. Repeat the signs taught during the previous week, and add three or four new signs.	Let several children take turns holding the book and "reading" the story with your help, if needed.	Let any children who did not get a turn to be the lead "reader" have the opportunity to do so. Sign the story, and encourage the children to sign, too.	Let the children "read" or tell the story while you act it out with puppets or stuffed animals on a small stage.	Let the children take turns playing roles in the puppet show; reading the story; or acting out the parts of the goats, troll, or frog.
Dramatic Play: Theme Area	Incorporate the puppet stage and puppets made by the children in the Art Area. They can act out the story on the bridge or use the puppet stage.	Add a picnic area to one side of the bridge, with a tablecloth, a picnic basket, plastic cups, plates, utensils, and plastic foods.	Repeat the story on the puppet stage and on the bridge, allowing the children to improvise as they play.	Repeat acting out the story, and encourage the children to assume new roles.	Have the children take turns performing the puppet show they have been practicing. Model how an audience should act.
Literacy Center	Continue to have the tape of the story and big book available. Have the children take home a letter asking their families to tell how they are brave and special.	Continue to have the tape of the story and big book available. Let children share their family shapes.	Continue to have the tape of the story and big book available. Let the children share their letters from home about how each is brave and special.	Continue to have the tape of the story and big book available. Continue to work on the Family Books.	Continue to have the tape of the story and big book available. Share each child's Family Book. Let them tell the story they have written.
Science and Math Center	Continue to work on the animal homes scene. Examine how the grass is growing in the different conditions.	Continue to work on the animal homes scene. Have the children show their individual gardens. Make a Seed Book.	Continue to work on the animal homes scene. Continue to work on the Seed Book. Examine, water, and discuss the gardens.	Continue to work on the animal homes scene, if needed. Continue to work on the Seed Book.	Finish the Seed Books. Have the children share their pages in the Seed Book with each other. Observe the gardens. Discuss what changes have taken place.
Art Area	Continue making the nature collages. Begin working on a mural of the story.	Hang the mural on the wall. Let the children paint a troll and billy goats on it. Have a variety of painting tools available.	Continue working on the mural. Let the children experiment with making goat hoof marks and troll footprints.	Continue working on and adding to the mural. Make paper bag puppets.	Let the children illustrate what they liked most about the story. Play different classical music as they work.
Sensory Area	Allow the children to continue playing in the exploration area. Explore size and texture.	Continue playing in the exploration area. Explore animal sounds. Record actual or human-generated animal sounds into the tape recorder.	Continue playing in the exploration area. Make faces. Pretend to be the billy goats, and walk through the grass, dirt, mud, and "river."	Continue playing in the exploration area. Repeat the tub texture activity. Add two or more tubs with mud. Let the children play with the mud.	Continue playing in the exploration area. Let the children whisper, talk, and shout into a tape recorder. Discuss the different levels of sounds.
Motor Area	Make a more complicated obstacle course. Include a troll. Have the children follow a rope woven in, around, and through objects to avoid the troll.	New challenges can be added to the obstacle course.	Add a climbing structure to the obstacle course.	Let the billy goats take turns leading other goats through the obstacle course using words as well as physical guidance.	Let the children make some changes to the obstacle course. Encourage creative changes. Have materials ready to stimulate new ideas.

From *Read, Play, and Learn!* by Toni W. Linder © 1999 by Paul H. Brookes Publishing Co., Inc.

TPBA | Play-Based | TPBI

TPBC

Play-Based Curriculum Planning Sheet: Storybook Activities

Date: Week Two   **Theme (optional):** Bravery/Family   **Book title (optional):** The Three Billy Goats Gruff

Play area	Monday	Tuesday	Wednesday	Thursday	Friday
Floor Play	Continue playing with and adding to the miniature scenario. Build bridges with blocks and cardboard.	Continue playing with and adding to the miniature scenario. Encourage children to create a story with materials.	Continue playing with and adding to the miniature scenario. Construct bridges, tunnels, and boxes.	Continue playing with and adding to the miniature scenario. Block play.	Continue playing with and adding to the miniature scenario. Continue block play. Do puzzles and play board games.
Table Play	Continue puppet stage play. Continue magnetic board play. Create and play the Troll Mouth game.	Repeat the Troll Mouth game. Continue puppet stage play. Continue magnetic board play. Let the children design characters using shapes.	Repeat making animals and characters from shapes. Continue puppet stage play. Continue magnetic board play.	Continue puppet stage play. Encourage the children to make up new stories. Continue magnetic board play. Make playdough.	Continue magnetic board play. Continue play with playdough. Continue puppet stage play.
Outdoor Play	Play Leap Frog in the grass. Make giant lily pads, and have the children jump like frogs from lily pad to lily pad. Free play.	Make a stuffed troll. Dress the troll and hang it from a tree or from swings. Let children take turns throwing a Nerf ball or tennis ball at the troll. Free play.	Play Troll, May I? Let the children draw trolls, goats, and bridges with sidewalk chalk. Free Play.	Make rubbings of various textures found outside. Free play.	Make homemade ice cream. Free play.
Snack	Oral motor: Practice animal hoof sounds. Do One Billy Goat fingerplay. Snack: Spinach pasta and milk	Oral motor: Pretend to be goats eating grass. Sing "Ten Little Billy Goats." Snack: Green beans and juice	Oral motor: Sing "Old MacDonald Had a Farm." Snack: Frogs on a log and water	Oral motor: Let children choose songs and fingerplays. Snack: Sliced cucumbers with crumbled feta cheese and juice	Oral motor: Let children choose songs and fingerplays. Snack: Goats' horns and juice
Books and Music					
Software					

From *Read, Play, and Learn!* by Toni W. Linder © 1999 by Paul H. Brookes Publishing Co., Inc.

TPBA   Play-Based   TPBI

TPBC

Play-Based

VOCABULARY

Labels

Bridge	Hand	Rocks
Brother	Herbivore	Saucer
Carnivore	Hill	Seed
Cave	Hillside	Sister
Checks	Hooves	Sky
Ears	Horns	Spear
Environment	Meadow	Tame
Eyes	Medal	Troll
Frog	Mountain	Valley
Goat	Paint	Wild
Grass	Poker	
Habitat	River	

Action Words

Color, coloring	Groan	Roar
Crash	Help	Scare
Creak	Jump	Send
Cross	Kick	Stop
Dislike	Like	Swinging
Eat	Play	Tramp
Feel	Poke	Wait
Gobble	Reel	Yield

Descriptors

Angry	Heavy	Quiet
Bad	High	Rough
Beyond	Hoarse	Sad
Big, bigger, biggest	Hungry	Scared, scary
Brave, bravely	Irritating	Scratchy
Cautious, cautiously	Little	Short, shorter, shortest
Down	Low	Small
Fearful	Mad	Smooth
First, second, third (ordinal numbers)	Mean	Soft
	Narrow	Soothing
Good	Nervously	Steep
Great	Noisy	Sticky
Greedy	Off	Sweet
Green	On	Tall, taller, tallest
Happy	Over	Tame
Hard	Pleasant	Thin

Through
Tiny
Ugly
Under

Unpleasant
Up
Warm
Wide

Wild
Youngest

MATERIALS

Toys and Equipment

Animal stamps
Baby Animal Lotto
Balance beam
Ball (large enough to kick)
Blocks
Card games
Card table
CD player
Classical music (tapes or CDs)
Climbing structure
Collapsible tunnel
Dice or spinner

Easels
Farm Friends Giant Floor Puzzle
Ice cream maker
Jump rope
Ladder
Lincoln Logs
Magnetic board and letters
Mats
Nerf ball or tennis ball
Plastic animal figures (goats and frogs)
Polaroid camera and film

Puzzles (with frogs and other outdoor animals)
Ramps
Sound book or See 'n Say
Stamp pads
Steps
Stuffed animals (goat puppets)
Tape recorder
Tinker Toys
Troll doll
Tubs
Wind-up or switch toys

Supplies

Animals' skin, hooves, skulls, and so forth (if possible)
Bags
Blanket (soft and green)
Bottle caps
Boxes
Brown paper
Brush (small and bristly)
Bundt or other doughnut-shaped cake or gelatin mold
Cans (empty)
Cardboard
Cardboard box
Clay
Cloth (pieces that are small and prickly)
Clothespins
Clothing (such as those worn by the billy goats and troll in the story)
Construction paper
Cookie cutters
Cord or clothesline
Cotton

Cotton swabs
Craft sticks
Crayons, markers, and pencils
Cups, plates, and utensils (plastic)
Dirt
Easter grass
Empty containers
Fabric scraps
Feathers
Felt (green)
Fingerpaints
Foam rubber
Fur pieces
Glue
Gold stars
Googly eyes
Hole punch
Ice bags
Leash
Leather articles (such as gloves, purses, belts, and shoes)
Liquid starch

Lunch bags (paper)
Magazines and catalogs (seed)
Magnets
Masking tape
Matting
Metal rings (for binding books)
Metal washers
Mirrors
Miscellaneous sets of items in three different sizes (lids, milk cartons, jars, buttons, etc.)
Nature items (things collected from outdoors)
Newspaper
Old shirt
Paint
Panty hose
Paper clips
Picnic basket
Pictures of animals and what they eat
Pictures of seeds sprouting

Pillows
Plastic cups, plates, and utensils
Plastic food
Plastic tubs
Plates (paper)
Popsicle sticks
Poster board (green)
Post-it notes
Ribbon
Rocks
Rope
Rough, prickly materials

Salad tongs
Sandpaper
Seed and garden catalogs
Seeds (grass, sunflower, bean, carrot, etc.)
Shallow pans
Shoebox
Sidewalk chalk
Sparkles
Sponges (green)
Stamps (rubber) of goats and frogs
Stickers

Sticks
Straws
String
Styrofoam meat trays
Tablecloth
Tadpoles
Three-ring binder
Tin cans (empty)
Toilet paper or paper towel tubes
Toothpicks
Twigs
Velcro

Food

Alfalfa sprouts
Bread (regular, cocktail size, French)
Bugles
Buns
Butter
Carrot juice
Carrots
Celery
Cheese spread/dip
Crackers
Cream cheese

Cucumbers
Feta cheese
Flour
Food coloring (green)
Fruit
Goat cheese
Green beans
Green peppers
Juice
Lettuce
Milk
Noodles (three different sizes)

Parmesan cheese
Peanut butter
Pigs in a blanket (hotdogs or sausages in rolls)
Pudding
Raisins
Salad dressing
Salt
Spinach pasta
Sugar
Vegetable juice
Vegetable oil

*See the sample ClickArt® at the end of the *Teacher's Guide*.

READING THE STORY

The use of symbols to represent bravery and sticking together to face scary things may help younger children to stay engaged with the story as well as help other children to remember the lessons the story teaches about fear, courage, and helping one another. Symbols might be stickers or stamps that show people holding hands or hugging. Other ideas might be "medals" for bravery and special charms that can protect the children. Then at the end of the reading each day, the children have a memento to remind them of these themes.

Day 1

Read the story to the children, and talk about times when they have been afraid. Talk about how sometimes when we are afraid we can talk ourselves into feeling braver, but sometimes we cannot. Talk about how at times when our fear is bigger, we look for help and comfort from someone else, like a mom, dad, brother, friend, grandparent, and so forth. Give each child a sticker that shows people together, and remind him or her how friends and families are there to help us feel safe. Let the children identify each of the characters in the story.

WEEK 1

Day 2

Read the story to the children showing them the pictures and allowing them to name the different goats, the troll, and the frog as they appear. Discuss what makes the troll so scary to each child. Discuss what is *not* scary about the troll (e.g., his pet frog, he hides under a bridge so maybe *he* is scared of something). Stamp the children's hands with a rubber frog stamp to remind them of their own "special friend" (whether it be a stuffed animal, blanket, toy, etc.) who helps them to feel safe when they are scared.

Day 3

Read the story again, and prompt the children to fill in the sounds that the goats make when crossing the bridge and the words that the troll says (e.g., "trip-trap, trip-trap," "Who's that tripping over my bridge?"). Write these phrases on separate pieces of paper; then hold them up while the children are saying them. Add a symbol for each so that the children will have a visual cue in addition to the print. For example, you might put two hooves next to "trip-trap, trip-trap" and a picture of a bridge next to "Who's that tripping over my bridge?" Talk about the brave people the children know and why they think they are brave (e.g., "My brother is brave because he walks to school all by himself"). Give each child a gold star as a medal for when he or she says something related to being brave.

Day 4
Read the story, and let the children fill in as many words as they can. Point to the words in the book as they are read. Prompt the children to act out the parts of the goats and the troll; encourage them to use different voices for the different parts that convey the youngest to oldest goats and the scary troll. Talk about when the children had someone help them when they were scared or when they helped someone else.

Day 5
Let the children "read" the story while you sign key words (e.g., GOAT, SCARY, BROTHER). Because many signs use gestures that resemble the word's meaning, signs can provide the children with another memory cue. Let the children take turns being each of the goats or the troll if they desire, and allow them to pretend to be that character as it comes up in the story. Give each child a small piece of synthetic fur, and tell them to feel how warm and soft it is, just like when we feel safe.

Day 1
Let the children tell the story and act out the parts. Repeat the signs taught during the previous week, and add three or four new signs. Encourage the children to sign certain key words as they tell the story. Talk about the grass that the goats eat and why they ran out of grass (lack of sun, water, and good soil). Talk about what the children like to eat. When reading the story, you may try substituting the sign for the oral word and see if the children can recognize the sign or remember the words from the story.

WEEK 2

Day 2
Let several children take turns holding the book and "reading" the story with your help, if needed. Talk about what frogs like to eat, and repeat what goats like to eat. Talk about how grass takes time to grow from seeds, frogs take time to grow from eggs, and goats take time to grow inside their mother's body.

Day 3
Let any children who did not get a turn to be the lead "reader" have the opportunity to do so today. You can sign the story and encourage and prompt the children to sign the key words, too. Have pictures of the signs with the words written out beneath them available for the children to see as the story is read.

Day 4
Let the children "read" or tell the story while you act it out with puppets or stuffed animals on a small stage. Provide the puppets and stuffed animals to the chil-

dren afterward so that they can act out whatever themes they are most interested in. Model the goat puppets or stuffed animals hugging as a family and sticking together when they are afraid.

Day 5   Let the children take turns playing roles in the puppet show; reading the story; or acting out the part of the goat, troll, or frog. Sign the story as the show goes on, and give children another "medal" for their bravery.

Sensorimotor Level

1. Children at the sensorimotor level may not follow the entire story or its more subtle themes of bravery and family, but they will enjoy the sounds of the animals and the scary voice of the troll.
2. Place a sticker or a stamp on each child's hand. Encourage these children to look at, take off, and put the stickers back on their body. Have the children feel the fur pieces, then rub them on their face, arms, and legs with the fur. Some children may resist having someone else rub their skin with this texture. Encourage tactile exploration by the children.
3. The children at this level will enjoy watching the puppet show. They may want to help with sound effects or to clap at the end.
4. Some of these children may learn some of the signs for the key words and will benefit from your or their peers' modeling. Signs provide an alternative means of communication for children who have difficulty with spoken language. Signing, when paired with speech, can also prompt actual speech.

Functional Level

1. In addition to all of the points at the sensorimotor level, children at the functional level may be ready to talk about simple labels and concepts (e.g., "goat," "green," "troll," "grass"). Modeling and emphasizing the prepositions as well as the sounds in some of the simple words will challenge these children.
2. Association of word patterns in the repetitive reading of the story will help these children develop a memory for words and short word sequences. As you read, leave silences for these children to try to fill in the missing word (e.g., "Trip-trap. Trip . . .").
3. Prompt these children to use longer sentences containing a subject, verb, and object (e.g., "The goat crossed the bridge").
4. Point to the words as they are read, and emphasize the cards that pair the written word with its picture or sign. The goal is not to teach these children to read the words but to associate the spoken word with print so that they will begin to understand that print has meaning.

Symbolic Level

1. Children at the symbolic level will display a range of emergent reading abilities. Observe each child's understanding of the concepts of *picture, story,* and *print.* As you involve each child, comment or ask him or her to comment in such a way that you are encouraging thinking and responding to each stimulus in a challenging manner.
2. Encourage these children to describe the characters and notice the details that give information about what the characters are like (e.g., "Tell me why you think the troll is mean. How can you tell?").
3. Encourage all of these children's attempts at reading or sounding out words.
4. The fun of reading the story is what is important for children at this level, rather than the process of trying to pair the correct sound with each letter.
5. Model and expand on the descriptions that these children offer. For example, if a child notes "Goats are eating grass," you might add, "Cows and horses eat grass, too. I wonder what that frog eats?"
6. Encourage these children to think beyond the immediate text. If the child says, "The little goat is scared, but he is crossing anyway," you might reply, "I wonder what would happen if he was too scared to cross. Then what?"
7. Children at this level should be praised for and encouraged in their attempts to read, regardless of their errors. Developing a sense of competence and autonomy will help encourage later efforts and success with more conventional reading.

DRAMATIC PLAY: THEME AREA

This area's activities are centered around a bridge crossing. A bridge can be constructed of steps leading up to a table and down the other side, with mats underneath and on both sides. The bridge should be high enough that children can play under it, but not so high as to be any real danger if a child jumps or falls onto the mats below. This will likely be easiest to set up in the Motor Area. Be sure to use the necessary bracing so that the bridge is stable and safe. Vary the access to the bridge from day to day by substituting steps with ramps and inserting other objects that must be climbed to cross to the other side. Clothing that is suggestive of that worn by the three goats and troll should be available and easily accessible near the bridge.

Day 1 Let the children play on and around the bridge, using the clothing to mimic the goats and troll. Do not expect the children to have internalized the story at this point. They may be more interested in the motor activity than anything else. You can model portions of the story, such as crossing the bridge while saying "Trip-trap, trip-trap. I'm crossing the bridge to get some green grass."

WEEK 1

Day 2 Facilitate the children's acting out the story, modeling new portions of the story if necessary. You might act the part of the troll, saying "I'm a hungry troll sitting under this bridge and fishing, waiting for someone to come across my bridge," as the children go over. Add the troll's pet frog (stuffed or plastic) on a leash to keep under the bridge.

Day 3 Allow the children to act out the story with support as needed. Incorporate the troll masks made in the Art Area.

Day 4 Have the children help make an obstacle course over and under the bridge and then act out the story as they choose, using the props and masks provided. Begin to fade facilitation. You may want to use the written signs from the Literacy Center (e.g., "Trip-trap!") to add meaningful print and help the children remember the line. Children are not expected to read the signs, but the signs will serve as a reminder of the story and its sequence. Some children may begin to recognize the word configurations, or you can prompt by pointing to the "tr" and saying, "trrr" as a sound–letter reminder.

Day 5 Incorporate into play the goat masks made in the Art Area. Encourage the children to take turns performing different parts as they play. Set up a fishing game under the bridge for the children playing trolls.

FISHING GAME

Cut out pieces of cardboard in the shape of fish, and glue a metal washer onto each fish. Attach string to a short stick, with a magnet at the end of the string. Children can "catch" the fish using magnets (which will connect with the metal washers) tied onto pieces of string.

Day 1 Incorporate the puppet stage and puppets made by the children in the Art Area. Children can act out the story on the bridge or use the puppet stage. You may need to model the use of the puppets by telling the story or acting out the story. Encourage the children to take turns as the storyteller and "actors."

Day 2 Add a picnic area to one side of the bridge, with a tablecloth; a picnic basket; plastic cups, plates, and utensils; and plastic foods from the House Area. Use empty wrappers and boxes so that the children can recognize and "read" the packages. Allow the children to act out the story and the picnic. Suggest catching fish to eat at the picnic. Take turns being the cook.

Day 3 Repeat the story on the puppet stage and on the bridge, allowing the children to improvise as they play. Some possibilities might be washing dishes in the river under the bridge, cooking different foods, taking a nap after the picnic, "reading" a book, and so forth.

Day 4 Repeat acting out the story, and encourage the children to assume new roles (e.g., director, storyteller, troll, frog). Encourage the children to use the language of the characters in the story.

Day 5 Have the children take turns performing the puppet show they have been practicing. Model how an audience acts as the children perform. Encourage the children to take turns acting out new roles.

Sensorimotor Level

1. The children at the sensorimotor level will enjoy the gross motor activity of crossing the bridge (crawling is appropriate for some), but they may not understand the relationship of their actions to the story. Encourage them to imitate the actions of their peers.
2. The soft puppets used in the Literacy Center can be used in this area to show these children simple themes, such as the goats hugging, running away from the troll, and having a picnic.

3. Point out and label different parts of the goat puppets (e.g., "horns," "eyes," "hooves") for these children, and ask them, "Where are *your* eyes?" (your feet, mouth, etc.), to extend the labeling.
4. These children will enjoy the sensory activities in the dramatization, such as washing the dishes, cooking, taking a nap, and so forth.

Functional Level

1. Sequencing and familiar routines will appeal to the children at the functional level; therefore, they will enjoy most of the above activities as well as the activities of the goats (e.g., crossing over the bridge, saying "trip-trap") and the troll (e.g., fishing).
2. Encourage these children to imitate the animals (e.g., hop like a frog across the bridge, "baaah" like a goat, tiptoe across the bridge like the baby goat).
3. These children will also enjoy the puppets and should be encouraged to participate in the puppet show.
4. Help these children compare the sizes of the puppets to determine which puppet corresponds to the "biggest" billy goat, the "tiniest," and so forth.
5. The props and costumes for each goat are important to enable children at this level to identify their character and prompt the words associated with the character and story sequence.
6. Encourage all language, regardless of whether it is accurate to the story. For some of these children, the "script" from the book will be an aid. Other children can be encouraged to say short comments at their own language level (e.g., "I'm hungry," "Don't eat me").

Symbolic Level

1. The children at the symbolic level will enjoy directing, storytelling, and acting out the parts in the story.
2. Encourage sequencing without prompting. Give these children wait time so that they can process and remember or improvise the story.
3. Your actions, reactions, suggestions, and questions can help move the children at this level along in many ways. For example, if a child declares that he or she will play the part of the oldest billy goat,

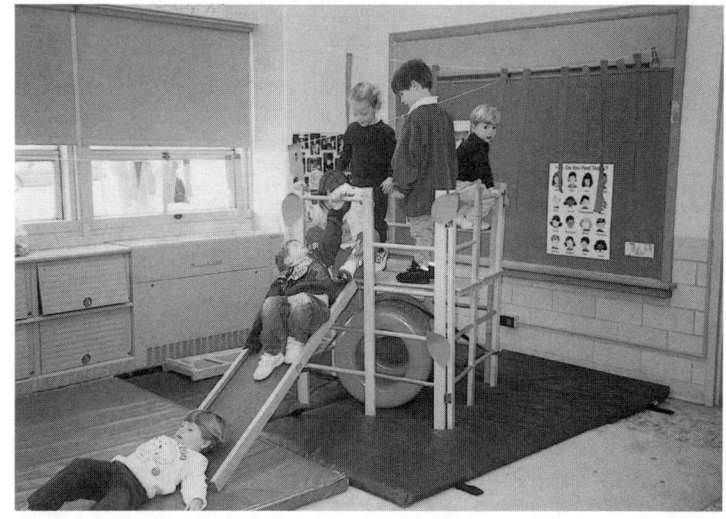

you might say, "If you are the biggest and oldest, would your voice be different? How would a big, tough billy goat talk?"

4. Add to these children's vocabulary. Describe how the goats walk (e.g., "cautiously," "nervously," "bravely").

5. Children at this level may need help with turn taking and cooperation. Help them to work out the differences that will inevitably accompany early efforts at cooperative work. Use problem-solving strategies that give the children, rather than the adult, the ability to make decisions (e.g., "You both want to be the big billy goat. Let's see if we can figure out a way you can both be the big billy goat. What ideas do you have?"). If the children have no ideas, you can allow them to retain decision-making ability by giving choices (e.g., "Let's see, we could have *two* big billy goats or you could take turns being the big goat"). Try using a sign-up sheet where children write their names (or you may help them) to sign-up for a turn at the different roles.

6. Encourage the children at this level to add language or revise the script or actions in creative ways. They may even want to add new scenes.

LITERACY CENTER

Day 1 Several activities in the 2-week period will require that the children bring materials from home, if possible. Children should participate at whatever level they can in the writing of the letter home requesting materials. This could be as simple as having the children watch you write the letter, with your modeling one use of print and the form and process of writing a letter. Having the children participate in any way will help to stimulate emergent literacy skills. Some children may want to write or draw on the letter to become more a part of the process. In these letters, include the following information:

- Have children bring pictures from home to make a Family Book. If they are not able to bring pictures, make magazines available so that children can cut out pictures to make the book. Pictures can include activities that the families enjoy and foods that they like to eat.
- Have the children bring a "special friend" from home (special toy or stuffed animal), and encourage them to take care of and protect their friend from scary things.
- Send home a blank piece of construction paper, cut into various shapes, for the children and their families to decorate together. Family members should trace their hands, write their names in the middle of the space, and then decorate the rest of the "family shapes" as they choose. This will help the children to talk about family as well as the size concepts of smaller to bigger.

Tape-record the story with different adults doing different voices for the three goats and the troll. Make a larger "book" of the story with copies of the pictures and larger print for the words. Laminate the pages, and place them in a three-ring binder. This will allow children of all levels to have access to the book without concerns of unintentional damage.

Day 2 Have the tape of the story and big book available. Begin work on the Family Books. Making a picture book with family members' pictures will help the children relate the characters in the story to their own lives. Begin to tape or glue pictures that the children have brought from home to blank pieces of paper for their Family Books. Have children dictate what caption should go beneath each picture. For some children this may be the name of the person or just "Daddy," whereas for other children it may be appropriate to encourage a caption that touches on themes in the story (e.g., "This is my sister. One time she was brave when she saw a spider. She didn't run away"). If a child's family does not send in pictures, you or the child can draw simple pictures of family members or cut out pictures from magazines. Discuss size concepts, such as *big, bigger, biggest; tall, taller, tallest;* and *short, shorter, shortest.* Make signs for the Dramatic Play: Theme Area, such as "bridge," "troll's cave," and "meadow."

Day 3   Continue to have the tape of the story and big book available. Continue to make the Family Books. Add pictures from magazines depicting activities that the children's families like and foods that they enjoy. Add captions as needed. Bind the books with yarn, and put each child's name on his or her book so that he or she has it to "read" throughout the module and can take it home at the end of the 2 weeks.

Day 4   Continue to have the tape of the story and big book available. As children bring back their "family shapes," encourage each child to tell about the drawings, designs, or decorations on the shapes (e.g., "This is my dad's hand, and it's biggest because he's tall"). Hang up the "family shapes" in a display, or combine them into a book that children and families can examine in a special setting in the room. Children whose families did not send back the shapes can trace their own hands on a shape and decorate it with drawings or pictures from magazines. As the children describe what is on the shape or banner, you can write down what the child says on a strip of paper for a caption. Let the child "read" his or her caption to other children at the center. Make more labels for the Dramatic Play: Theme Area, such as "rocks," "frog," "river," and so forth.

Day 5   Continue to have the tape of the story and big book available. Take Polaroid pictures of each child's "special friend." Paste these on a piece of paper, and have the children dictate a caption about what their friend is afraid of and about how the child protects or takes care of his or her friend (e.g., "This is my bear, Brownie. He's afraid of the dark. I sleep with him and he feels better"). You should also bring a special friend to share. Any child will, however, repeat what another child said unless you assist each child in thinking of new words or phrases. One option is for you to make available magazine pictures of scary things to stimulate ideas, such as snakes, lightning and thunder, monsters, and so forth. You can write the children's words on the paper so that they can "read" them back to their friends. Place a line under each word and point to it as you read the words back to the child. The line should be distanced from the word so that it is clearly visible. The lines will help the child see that one word is said for each word that is written. The pauses between words are, thus, made more visible, and the child more easily follows the spoken word and associated print.

Day 1   Continue to have the tape of the story and big book available. Write a letter for the children to take home with them. Ask the families to tell about how their child is brave and special. Encourage the family to be creative, and let them know that their phrase or story will be read aloud in their child's class.

WEEK 2

Because the children helped to write the letter, they will be more likely to make sure their families read it. Although the children should determine the actual words to be used, the letter might look something like this:

Dear Mom and Dad,

We are reading *The Three Billy Goats Gruff*. The three billy goats were brave when they crossed the bridge. There was a mean troll underneath. The biggest billy goat protected his brothers. In class we are talking about being brave. Please write down how I am brave and special so that my teacher can tell the class.

Dear [teacher's name],

My child _____ is brave when _____.

My child is special because _____.

When _____ is afraid, I make him/her feel better by

_____.

Thanks, Mom and Dad. I think you are special, too!

Love,

P.S. Please read to me what you write down so that I can tell my friends.

If some of the parents in the class cannot read, you may call the parents and fill out the form on the telephone. In this way, all of the children have something to share. Make tickets and programs for the puppet show (see Table Play).

Day 2   Continue to have the tape of the story and big book available. Share the special family shapes (sent home at the beginning of Week 1 to be decorated together) from home, and let each child participate in the telling about the pictures and writing on the shape. Add new shapes to the display area. Continue sharing the children's special friends and fears. This time you can have strips of paper with pictures and phrases about people or things that help them to be brave, pictures of family members, pictures of stuffed animals, pictures of people hugging, and so forth. You can help children match the pictures or phrases about their fears with the pictures and phrases of how they cope with the fears. These can be posted on a bulletin board, along with the children's names. This process should not be forced. Let the children look at the pictures and talk about them. You may support the conversation by commenting, adding information, talking about your own fears and brave actions, and so forth. This should be a conversation and game, not a structured assignment. Continue to make tickets and programs for puppet performances.

Day 3   Continue to have the tape of the story and big book available. As the letters are returned, let the children share their letters from home about how they are brave and special. Let each child tell what he or she thinks the letter says before reading it. As the child watches, you can slowly read each letter and underline the words. Let each child add the letter to his or her Family Book.

Day 4 Continue to have the tape of the story and big book available. Continue to work on the Family Books. Read the letters from home.

Day 5 Continue to have the tape of the story and big book available. Share each child's Family Book, allowing the children to tell the story they have written about their family.

Sensorimotor Level

1. Children at the sensorimotor level can relate more to three-dimensional figures than two-dimensional pictures. Have animal pictures and figures available to represent the characters in the book. Compare the figures with the pictures.
2. Have sounds that represent characters available as well. This could be accomplished by different audiotapes that the children can play in the recorder—animal sounds and a music tape with animal songs. Also, make sure that these children can easily operate the tape recorder. A simple stop–go switch may be added.
3. Adding different colored stickers to the tape recorder's "play" and "stop" buttons (green and red) may help some of these children differentiate which button to push.
4. Provide a variety of writing materials for children at this level, including crayons, markers, and pencils. Let them experiment with making marks on paper along with the other children.
5. Some of these children may be able to point to and name family members. (Make sure parents label the pictures so that you can assist the child in naming the people in their family pictures.)
6. Place these children's hands on the hand silhouette on the family shapes. Label these "hand."

Functional Level

1. The children at the functional level will be attempting many early reading behaviors. You can encourage them to look at and label the characters and actions in the story.
2. Model following the story with your finger in the big book as the tape plays.
3. Some of these children may imitate your "reading" the story to younger children.
4. Let these children scribble or "write" under the pictures in their Family Books. You can ask them what their marks "say," and write the transcription beneath so that these children see the association between what is on the paper and the words being spoken.

5. Children at this level will enjoy playing with the animal figures and may engage in more sequencing during their play. Encourage these children to develop more complex sequences through modeling and joining in the play.

6. Have these children look at the hands and designs on the family shapes. Describe the hands using the word "big" and "small."

Symbolic Level

1. Children at the symbolic level will enjoy the activities described for the previous two levels and may also begin to demonstrate higher levels of emergent literacy as they show more interest in trying to read conventionally. Encourage these children to experiment with "reading" and writing.

2. Some of these children may have a sight word (word they can recognize on sight by the letters and configuration). The predictable nature of *The Three Billy Goats Gruff* allows the children to remember and associate sounds, words, and print. You can assist by directing the children's attention to the sounds and words as they say them.

3. Allow these children to explore the reading and writing materials in ways with which they are comfortable, but also encourage them to try new things and learn new concepts by making associations between what they know and what they may be ready to master. For example, some children at this level may recognize their own name and may be able to write it as well. You may point out other words that contain the same letters and sounds.

4. These children should be encouraged to be more independent as they "read" their Family Books and other materials.

5. As with the children at the previous levels, you should encourage these children to write. Children at this level may use the materials to "write" their own stories or cards independently. All efforts should be encouraged and praised. You can ask what the writing says and write the transcription below the marks the child has made.

SCIENCE AND MATH CENTER

Day 1   Begin working on a class grass garden. Prior to class, make a picture chart to illustrate the steps. Plant grass seeds in a shallow pan for the class to monitor as they grow over the next few weeks. Several experiments will be done to show the effect of depriving grass of light or water. Have the children begin working on individual grass gardens, too. Provide each child with a cup. Assist the children in writing their names on their cups (or write their names for them). Give each child a scoop of potting soil to put in the cup. Then provide each child with a variety of grass seeds. Assist each child in planting the seeds, while talking about how the seeds will swell and grow with water, light, and warm soil. Have pictures of how seeds sprout at the table for the children to refer to as the days pass.

Play matching games with colors, shapes, and numbers using stickers of frogs and goats. (Stickers can be made by the children using Post-it notes and animal stamps and stamp pads.) Add the stickers to the shape, color, and number puzzle pieces. The stickers will give the children new interest in old materials. They will also encourage the children to look at two attributes (picture and shape) and choose the most important one.

Day 2   Make number puzzles. Draw the numbers 1–10 on pieces of 8½" x 11" poster board or construction paper (one number to each piece). Cut out the numbers prior to class. Let the children place the corresponding number of pictures, stickers, or stamps on each number (e.g., four stamps on the number 4). Let the children decorate and color the numbers. Later you can laminate each number and cut each into the number of pieces that corresponds to the number (e.g., cut the number 10 into 10 pieces.) Cut the pieces so that one stamp, sticker, or picture is on each piece.

Play the Foods that Animals Eat matching game. Have the children match food with animals (e.g., grass to goats, hay to horses, mice to owls). Talk about concepts related to what animals eat (e.g., *herbivore, carnivore, tame, wild*). Provide pictures of animals that the children can glue onto a chart. Make separate "food" pieces to be glued onto smaller individual squares. Laminate all of the pieces. Glue small Velcro pieces to each set so that when the children place the food piece on the animal on the chart, they stick together. (Velcro can be omitted if the chart is not hung on the wall.) Repeat the matching game with colors, shapes, and numbers. Water the grass gardens.

Day 3   Bring a tadpole to class. Show the tadpole to the children, and discuss how it will grow into a frog. Have pictures showing each stage of growth. Talk about the characteristics of the tadpole and the characteristics of the frog. Which characteristics are the same? Which are different? Have the children discuss how they think the troll in the story got his frog.

Continue to observe the grass gardens. The grass may have started to sprout by now. Cover one part of the class garden with an upside-down opaque cup. Explain to the children that the grass under the cup will not grow very well without light, as they will see in the coming days. Cover another section of the garden with an upside-down clear glass. Explain how the glass cover will keep more water in the soil and more warmth inside from the sun, so the grass under this glass will grow faster than the rest of the grass. Keep one section of the tray dry so that the children can see what will happen when the grass does not get any water.

Let the children play with the number puzzles that they made the previous day. You can help them use one-to-one correspondence by encouraging them to count the number of pieces and the number of animals on each puzzle. Label the animals and the name of the number as the children put together the puzzle.

Day 4   Continue to play the Foods that Animals Eat matching game. Assist the children by giving clues or hints, if their first choice is incorrect. Play the Smallest to Biggest game. Provide three different sizes of pasta noodles (or other food) all mixed together in a large bowl. Provide three labeled containers that are similarly graded into small, medium, and large sizes. Children can experiment with putting the noodles in the corresponding size container. You can make a game out of sorting by letting the children pretend to be trolls and billy goats. The child who is playing the troll says, "Who is crossing my bridge?" The child next to him or her is the billy goat and says "I am." The troll replies, "I want _____ [big, medium, small, or other size-relational word] food!" The child playing the billy goat then chooses a noodle and places it in a corresponding cup. If the right size food went into the right size container, you can say, "Trip-trap! Trip-trap!" If the child is incorrect, you can say, "Try again, billy goat." When the correct match is made, you can say, "Trip-trap! Trip-trap!" and then the child who was the goat becomes the troll and asks the next child, "Who's crossing my bridge," and so forth. Small "goat" and "troll" figures may be added, if available, and passed to the children as a reminder of roles. Continue to observe the gardens and note the changes in the grass. Water the grass.

Day 5   Using the fish and fishing poles made in the Dramatic Play: Theme Area, play Fishing Bingo. Draw numbers, shapes, or letters on the fish, and make laminated Bingo cards (or purchase manufactured ones) that correspond to simple or more complex matching. Let the children attach a paper clip to each fish (this demands fine motor skills) so that the magnet on the fishing line can "catch" the fish. Let several children take turns "fishing" to complete their Bingo cards. Although this game requires some preliminary work on your part, the addition of fishing to the common Bingo game allows the children to attempt to look for what they need on their card, look for the corresponding fish, and use visual-motor skills to attempt to hook the fish. This makes a game of chance into a more complex cognitive and motor activity.

Begin working on creating an animal homes scene. This project will take several days to complete and should be done on the floor and left out so that all of the children can see the scene as it progresses. Provide pictures of different animals as well as different materials that represent those used for animals' homes (e.g., twigs and string for nests, grasses and clay to make burrows, Popsicle sticks for "wooden" planks to make a barn). Before adding the pictures of animals and so forth, let the children first paint grass, sky, and trees on a mural on the floor. Let the children choose which animals they want in the scene. They may get ideas from pictures you provide, or they may enjoy looking through magazines of animals to see what they like. Let the children cut out the animal pictures and make their homes on the scene with materials you provide or with materials the children gather on the playground. Help them to think about why the animals they selected live where they do, what they will need to make its home, and how to find the materials and assemble their animal's home. Children love to use big words, so use words such as "environment," "habitat," and so forth to expand the vocabulary in those children who are ready for these concepts.

Day 1 Continue to work on the animal homes scene. Examine how the grass is growing in the different conditions. Discuss how light, water, and heat affect the grass. Repeat the Smallest to Biggest game with the troll and the billy goats.

WEEK 2

Day 2 Continue to work on the animal homes scene. Have the children show their individual grass gardens and talk about what colors their grasses are, how big their grass is, and so forth. Discuss the differences in the different types of grass. Read the names of the different types of grass. Review the process of sprouting seeds that is posted.

Make a Seed Book. This project may take several days. Provide the children with several different types of seeds that are easily recognized (e.g., sunflower, bean, carrot). Provide garden magazines or seed catalogs that show these plants so that some of the children can cut out pictures if they would like. Some children may prefer to color or paint pictures instead. On a piece of poster board, have each child glue his or her seeds and picture of what the seeds will become. Write the name of each seed on each page. Bind the pages with yarn or metal rings, and make the book available for the children to read and for the parents to examine.

Day 3 Continue to work on the animal homes scene. Continue to work on the Seed Book. Let the children "read" and explain their pages in the book. Examine, water, and discuss the grass gardens. Repeat the Smallest to Biggest game with the troll and the billy goats.

Day 4 Continue to work on the animal homes scene, if needed. Continue to work on and "read" the Seed Book. Repeat the Smallest to Biggest game with the troll and the billy goats. Make sure all of the children have a chance to play the different games if they have not had the opportunity.

Day 5   Finish the Seed Book. Give the children the opportunity to share their pages in the Seed Book with one another in pairs. Let each of the children show and talk about the pages they created. Review the class grass garden, and discuss what changes have taken place: Which grass has grown the best? Why? Let the children describe what has happened to the tadpole to their peers.

Sensorimotor Level

1. Although many of the more advanced science concepts may be beyond some of these children, children at the sensorimotor level will enjoy the textures of the dirt, grass, seeds, and materials used for making the animal homes scene.
2. Provide plastic frogs and goats that are labeled for these children. Show the children the animals compared with pictures of real animals.
3. Some of the matching and sorting games will be of interest to children at this level as well. They will be more interested, however, in the process of putting things into a container and taking them out than in discriminating differences.
4. Help these children internalize the labels of different animals and concepts by talking about the different projects, seeds, plants, and animals. Showing them the same animals in the different places in the room will help them to internalize the labels of different animals and concepts.
5. Children at this level may also enjoy turning pages in the magazines and looking at the pictures, even if they do not recognize the animals.

Functional Level

1. The children at the functional level will enjoy all of the activities for children at the sensorimotor level. In addition, these children may try to cut out pictures. Label the animals' names and point out their characteristics (e.g., "This goat has horns") to these children.
2. The work of gluing the seeds to the paper and playing in the dirt while making the gardens may be interesting for children at this level. Label the sizes of the seeds. Help these children follow the pictures on the picture chart for planting the seeds. Label the actions that they are performing.
3. These children will be interested in the characteristics of the materials for the animal homes scene. You can help the children see the relationship between the materials and the animals. Talk about where the animals live and what they eat.

4. When children at this level are playing with the number puzzles or the matching games, guide their observations of the key aspects that they need to see, the similarities and differences, and the relationship between the parts and the whole. Provide just enough guidance so that they can see the relationship and then solve the problem.
5. These children may not be able to catch the "right" fish but should be encouraged to catch any fish and label what they have caught.
6. Show these children how the tadpole matches a certain picture on the tadpole growth chart.

Symbolic Level

1. The children at the symbolic level will likely enjoy Fishing Bingo as well as many of the matching games that use higher concepts and numbers. Some of these children may be able to try to catch their fish in numerical order.
2. The puzzles of different numbers will interest these children. Pair these children with children at a functional level so that they will use their language to explain what they are doing and facilitate their friend's play.
3. Involve these children in the planning of the animal homes scene. Have them discuss what they will need to make the homes for these animals.
4. Let these children help set up the materials for the project.
5. Discuss with these children the characteristics of the different types of seeds and grasses.
6. Have these children observe the growing grass and tadpole and make predictions about how and when each will change. Discuss why frogs need legs and what would happen if the tadpole never grew legs.
7. If one of these children becomes particularly interested in a topic, such as the seeds, the tadpole, the animal homes, and so forth, let him or her pursue independent research by looking at additional books and resources related to the topic.
8. Some of these children may choose to make more books, puzzles, and so forth. Encourage such motivation by providing more materials and options.

ART AREA

Many of the activities in the Art Area allow children to choose from many different materials. The provision of an "art cart," a rolling cart with containers filled with different utensils and decorative items, will encourage creativity and making choices.

Day 1

Show the children how to make creative troll masks out of cardboard pieces or paper plates. Cut ovals or circles the size of a child's face from the center of the round cardboard pieces (or paper plates). Save the cutout pieces for big ears or a nose, and use the remaining oval or circle face "frames" for the troll masks. Glue a Popsicle stick to the bottom of the face frame for a handle. Have a variety of materials available to decorate the front of the mask like the scary troll (e.g., yarn, ribbon, noodles, or string for the hair; crayons, markers, or sparkles for the ears). A piece of construction paper can be used to create a scary nose by folding it into a cone and then taping it together. Staple yarn to each side of the nose so that it can be tied around the child's head. When ready, the children can hold up the masks and peer through the opening in the face frame.

Day 2

Make goat masks the same way that you made the troll masks, only with cotton for a beard and hair. Make pointed ears and/or horns out of the leftover pieces of cardboard or paper plates. These masks can now be used in the Dramatic Play: Theme Area as props in the dramatization. Finish making the troll masks.

Create and decorate the troll's cave. Let the children paint a cardboard box "cave" or a piece of cloth that will go over a card table. Let them stuff paper sacks with newspaper, tape them closed, and paint them to look like rocks. Use Easter grass to decorate the inside of the cave. Let the children glue some of the grass around the outside of the cave. When the cave is complete, add it to the Dramatic Play: Theme Area. Using the items made in the Art Area in the Dramatic Play: Theme Area will encourage the children to participate in both activities.

Day 3

Let the children draw or design goats or trolls. Give all of the children construction paper, and let them select materials from the art cart. When completed, label them with the child's name and his or her description of the picture. As the children finish the pieces, you can encourage the children to arrange them by size into small, medium, and large goat sequences. Have the children paste a precut paper or matting board frame around their art pieces for display. Artwork that is displayed with such care will show the children that their efforts are valued.

Continue making goat masks.

Day 4   Make three-dimensional goats from a variety of objects. Cardboard toilet paper or paper towel tubes make a good body for the goat. Toothpicks can make legs for the toilet paper tube bodies, and straws can be used for the paper towel tube bodies. (Of course, other objects and combination are also interesting!) Show the children how the toothpicks or straws can be poked into the tube on one side for legs. (Use a hole puncher before putting in the straws.) Add a toothpick or shorter straw on top of the tube, at one end, for a neck. A twist-off bottle cap; construction paper cut in the shape of a goat head; or a grape, strawberry, or other piece of fruit can be used as a head attached to the tooth-pick neck. The children can then glue on "goat hair" made from cotton, fuzzy white (or other goat color) cloth, yarn, or Halloween spider web material. Add googly eyes to the head. Label each of the children's goats with their names, as they will be very proud of them. Discuss the body parts and characteristics of goats as you make them.

Day 5   Continue making three-dimensional goats. Some children may take more time to finish this project than others. Other children may want to make another goat of another size or composition. Encourage creative experimentation.

Create nature collages. Explain how the children can make a nature collage using objects they have collected from outdoors. Let each child squeeze a puddle of white glue onto the middle of a Styrofoam meat tray. Each child can then select from the items collected (e.g., pebbles, bark, leaves, nuts, pine needles, pine cones, seeds, shells, dried weeds) and arrange them on a base piece of driftwood, bark, or rock. Have the children dab the item with glue by using a craft stick or cotton swab that has been dipped in the puddle of glue to encourage use of precise fine motor skills, or the child may also choose to dip the item in the puddle of glue. Let the children continue adding more bits of things from nature and attaching them to the base with glue. Label each nature collage with the child's name. Allow the collage to dry overnight before touching.

Day 1   Continue making the nature collages with those children who want to continue this project. Begin working on a mural of the story. Lay the mural on the floor for this part. Give the children sponges to paint the grass and the sky. Let the children paint and then glue Popsicle sticks onto the paper to make a bridge. Let the children cut small pieces of green yarn or cut fringe on green paper for grass. They can then glue these onto the mural. **WEEK 2**

Day 2   Hang the mural on the wall. Let the children paint a troll and billy goats (do not worry if there are too many) on it. Have a variety of painting tools available for the children. In addition to brushes, have feathers, markers, cotton balls, foam rubber, and so forth. This will encourage the children to experiment and try new ways of painting.

Day 3

Continue working on the mural. Add cotton or other materials to the goats. Discuss why it is difficult to make the heavier items stick to the paper. Let the children experiment with making goat hoof marks and troll footprints with fingerpaints. One way to make hooves is to bend the first two fingers and paint the hooves with the part of the fingers between the first and second knuckles. "Footprints" can be made with the side of the hand when the fist is clenched or the palms of the hands and then add the toes with the tips of the thumb and fingers. Encourage the children to try to figure out other ways to make hooves and feet with their hands and fingers (or feet and toes).

Day 4

Continue working on and adding to the mural. Continue fingerpainting goat hoof marks and troll footprints. Let the children experiment with drawing on the fingerpaint with tools, such as a straw, a feather, or other hard and soft objects.

Make paper bag puppets. Open a paper lunch bag, and stuff it with crumpled newspaper. Tie the bag closed with string about one third of the way from the bottom to make the neck (leaving about two thirds of the sack for the face). Be sure to leave enough room inside, though, to put three fingers up through the neck. Position the bag so that the head end is up and the neck end is down. Have the children draw or glue on scary troll features. Then have them put their fingers in the neck to control it. A simpler puppet can also be made using a lunch bag without stuffing. Children who prefer to do so can paint or decorate the sack and then just put a hand inside.

Day 5

Let the children illustrate what they liked most about the story. Have a variety of materials available for the children to use (e.g., easel and paper, paper and scissors, crayons, markers, and so forth). Play different types of classical music while the children work on their artwork. Ask them to tell you when the music sounds like a troll, a little billy goat, and so forth. Discuss how the characters would sound different.

Sensorimotor Level

1. Encourage the children at the sensorimotor level to explore and use different tools to make the collage or goats, even though they may not understand the meaning of the collage.
2. These children may enjoy putting their fingers in the fingerpaint and playing in it. If the children mouth objects, let them use pudding paint (pudding used as fingerpaint) instead.

3. Children at this level will most likely not be interested in making the masks. Have these children hold the masks made by the other children up to their faces and look at themselves in the mirror.
4. Label the materials being used "rock," "paint," and so forth. Children at this level will not understand the representations the other children are creating, so labeling body parts, such as "head" and "legs," on the goats will be confusing.
5. Encourage children at the sensorimotor level to compare the textures of materials.

Functional Level

1. The children at the functional level will be able to associate the troll masks they make with the trolls in the story. You can point out the similarities between the troll mask and the troll in the story.
2. When fingerpainting on the mural, have these children point out different aspects of a scene by following your lead: "This is the sky, mountain, grass"; or, "What kind of animal is this?"
3. Encourage children at this level to compare textures, colors, sizes, and shapes of materials.
4. Encourage the development of representational and symbolic thought by pointing out the two-dimensional and three-dimensional characteristics of their art and how they are like the pictures or actual animals.

Symbolic Level

1. Involve the children at the symbolic level in the process of planning the collage. They can help pick out the different objects to place on the collage. They can also explain to others how to put together and design the collage.
2. Arrange picture charts for these children on how to make masks. Picture charts will allow these children to practice sequential picture reading. Label the pictures with words, and then read the words to the children while explaining the process.
3. Children at this level are beginning to represent their world symbolically. They can be given guidance in how to draw body parts and aspects of nature. You can facilitate by pointing out the characteristics of the objects (e.g., "The head is like a small oval, and the body is like a large oval") and demonstrating how shapes and textures help make their drawing look more realistic (e.g., painting the billy goat's coat with a feather). The goal is not to make exact replicas, but to help the children see relationships and be able to express visually their cognitive understanding.

SENSORY AREA

The Sensory Area for this module focuses on helping children distinguish the difference between bravery and fear. Rather than place the children in fear-inducing situations, however, the area can be supplied with materials that create comfort and discomfort. For example, comfort and feeling good about yourself and your actions can be used to signify bravery. Have available an exploration area where children can explore things that are comfortable and things that are uncomfortable. Comfort can be provided with materials such as soft stuffed animals, big pillows, blankets for warmth and softness, and a comfortable tight space to squeeze into so as to stimulate deep pressure and a sense of security. Ice bags can be provided to simulate chills and cold discomfort: how you might feel with a sense of fear. Rough surfaces such as prickly cloth, coarse sandpaper, and a small bristly brush can be used to discuss the unpleasant feeling of a scary situation. This exploration space should remain available throughout the 2 weeks.

Day 1 With a picture chart as a guide, assist the children in making the stretchy green grass. Make a picture chart of the following sequence.   **WEEK 1**

STRETCHY GREEN GRASS

Mix equal parts of regular glue and liquid starch (depending on how much you want to make). Add green food coloring. Let the children stir the mixture, first with a spoon, then with their hands. Let the mixture sit overnight. Like magic it will become stretchy grass!

Day 2 Let the children experiment with the stretchy grass they made the previous day. They can pull it, cut it, squeeze it, and stretch it into strings with a friend. Explore different ways to make the "trip-trap" sound. Some methods include lightly slapping your cheeks while your mouth is open, slapping a bare leg and a clothed leg, lightly slapping the chest, stomping feet on a hollow surface, banging empty cans on a surface, or slapping hands on a hollow surface. The use of timing is essential to gaining an adequate clip-clop sound effect, so this activity also encourages children to listen for sound intervals. You can model or let individual children lead the trials. Discuss how the sounds differ. Ask the children how they can make a loud "trip-trap" sound. What makes the best soft clip-clop sound? Which sounds would the big-, medium-, or small-size goats make with their hooves? Make this into a game by letting different children think of ways to make the "trip-trap" sounds using their bodies or materials in the area.

Day 3   Create a texture game. Make a grid on a large piece of poster board. (You may want grids of different sizes, 2 x 2, 4 x 4, 6 x 6, depending on the abilities of the children. Start with a small 2 x 2 grid.) In each square, glue an item with a different texture related to the story. Also in each square, place or draw a picture of the item and the printed label. Possible textures include grass, bark, straw, and leaves, which are also consumed by goats; and sand, rocks, sticks, and moss (as it grows on rocks or wet wood), which all could be found in or near a river like the one in the story. Have a separate set of actual items available. After each child has examined the items, place the second set into a texture bag or feely bag. Each child can then reach in, feel, and guess (by naming or pointing to the matching picture on the grid) what the item is before pulling it out. The child can then place the item on the appropriate square on the grid. Point out how the real object is like the picture but is also different in appearance and feel. Have the children describe the items with adjectives, such as "rough," "hard," "scratchy," "soft," "smooth," and so forth.

Some children may enjoy continuing making "trip-trap" sounds.

Day 4   Allow the children to continue playing in the exploration area with comfortable and uncomfortable materials. You can expand the children's descriptive vocabulary by labeling the feelings associated with the textures with different "feeling" words, such as "pleasant," "unpleasant," "feels good," "feels bad," "soothing," "irritating," "like," "dislike," and so forth.

Repeat the texture game from yesterday, or you can modify the game to make it a texture relay. Today you may want to name a texture known to be in the bag, and encourage a child to run to the bag, reach in and find that texture, grab it, run back to the beginning point, and place the item on the matching square on the grid.

Day 5   Allow the children to continue playing in the exploration area with comfortable and uncomfortable materials and to continue playing with the textures.

Explore the skin, hooves, horns, skulls, leather, and so forth of different animals. Some such items may be obtainable through the children's families, through a collection from a local school, or through a local parks department traveling display. Leather can be in the form of gloves, purses, belts, and shoes. Have pictures available of the animals that are associated with each item. Have reference books available with pictures of actual materials as well.

Day 1   Allow the children to continue playing in the exploration area with comfortable and uncomfortable materials. Explore size and texture. The activity can begin with a picture of each of the billy goats showing their relative size. Discuss how each size relates to the others, by holding each picture up next to the others. Have sets of other objects, with different textures, that can be ordered in the same way. Items such as milk cartons, spoons, lids, jars, buttons, toy cars, and blocks are examples of materials that can be sequenced by size.

WEEK 2

This activity facilitates the development of visual and tactile discrimination; eye–hand coordination; ability to place objects in sequential order; and, if diverse objects are mixed together, classification.

Day 2   Allow the children to continue playing in the exploration area with comfortable and uncomfortable materials. Explore sounds of different animals. The sounds of a goat are different from those of a sheep, a horse, a cow, or a pig. These animals sound different when they are distressed and when they are relaxed. A guessing game could be made by imitating the sounds of each of the animals and asking which animal makes the sound and whether it is scared or happy. The sound of an animal's voice when scared can rise in pitch, become more rapid, and/or become louder. Record actual or human-generated animal sounds into a tape recorder. The children can then determine whether the animal is happy, hungry, sad, mad, and so forth. Of course, it is not important that the children identify the "right" emotion but, rather, that they listen carefully and learn to discriminate sounds. Let the children try to make different types of animal noises into the tape recorder. Playing a card game, in which children turn over a card with an animal on it and make that animal's sound to win the card, can enforce picture–sound connection.

Day 3   Allow the children to continue playing in the exploration area with comfortable and uncomfortable materials. Practice making scared, mean, fearful, happy, and brave faces. Show the children pictures of people displaying these emotions, and let them try to imitate the pictures in front of a mirror. Each child can have a photograph taken of him or her making a face. Label each photograph with the child's name and the emotion that he or she is expressing. The photographs can then be mounted on a bulletin board or placed in a photo album for the children to examine later.

Place four tubs on the floor in a line. At the end of the line of tubs, place several towels. In the first tub, put enough cut grass to make a thick pad when stepped on. In the second tub, place dirt; in the third tub, make mud; and in the fourth tub, pour water. Let the children remove their shoes and be billy goats walking through the grass, dirt, mud, and "river." Encourage the children to label the sensory material and their actions and to talk about how each sensation feels. If they are not yet at this level, provide a model (e.g., "You are stomping through the grass. The grass feels soft").

Day 4   Allow the children to continue playing in the exploration area with comfortable and uncomfortable materials. Repeat the tub textures activity from yesterday. The children can also explore the textures with their hands. In addition to or instead of the previous day's activity with four different materials in tubs, place dirt in one or more tubs. Add water so that the dirt becomes mud. (Make sure that the mud is moist but not sloppy.) Place different tools, shapes, cookie cutters, and so forth next to the tubs. Let the children play in the mud and experiment with making different prints. Talk about the prints that are left in the mud after it rains.

Day 5   Allow the children to continue playing in the exploration area with comfortable and uncomfortable materials. Let the children whisper, talk, and shout into a tape recorder. Talk about how a whisper is "quiet" and is a "little" sound, talking is "not too loud" and is a "middle-size" sound, and shouting is "noisy" and is a "big" sound. Have the children experiment with making noises that are labeled with these adjectives (e.g., "Let's see if you can make a sound that is not too loud").

Sensorimotor Level

1. If children at this level do not initiate exploration, first encourage them to observe and imitate their peers. If this is unsuccessful, you may want to gradually and gently put their fingers into different materials. Show enthusiasm, and model pleasurable exploration.
2. Children at this level may be preverbal or nonverbal. Therefore, their responses to ice or different textures may be preverbal or nonverbal. Attach words to their sounds or expressions that these children may imitate (e.g., "Ugh!" "Yuck!" "OOO!").
3. Children at this level may not differentiate sizes. Place items of two different sizes next to each other. Label the items, emphasizing the size adjective (e.g., "I need the *big* spoon"). If the child is not yet at this level, use two different items rather than two different sizes of the same item. Make this meaningful and fun for the child by making it into a hiding and finding game.
4. When the "trip-trap" sounds are made, let these children imitate the actions that produce the sounds. The combination of sounds and actions should make this fun for these children.
5. At this level, children are learning to label their own body parts. As you make noises for the "trip-trap" sounds, label the body parts being used (e.g., cheeks, hands, legs).
6. While these children are making animal sounds, draw their attention to the shape of their faces. When making happy, sad, brave, and scared faces, use a mirror to facilitate looking and focusing on the details. Pair the faces with appropriate sounds to make this more fun. The children at this level may not understand the relationship between the label and the facial expression, but they can watch and imitate some of the actions and sounds. Being able to imitate facial gestures and movements is an important skill for speech sound production.
7. Use of a sound book or a See 'n Say toy with animal sounds may be helpful in connecting pictures in books, actual sounds, and imitated voicing.

Functional Level

1. All of the points for children at the sensorimotor level apply to the children at the functional level as well.
2. Children at this level benefit from repetition to reinforce concepts and actions. Repeat actions several times with verbal cues and labels.
3. Emphasize with these children turn taking in each of the activities to promote language and social skills.
4. The words the children use to describe the feel of different materials can be written down, facilitating the oral–written link. Children at this level will not yet be able to decipher words, but they may begin to recognize that print is related to speech.
5. Children at this level will benefit from exploring many different textures. Present many examples of a texture that can be labeled with the same adjective. For example, a pillow, a tissue, and a cotton ball are "soft"; a friend's hand, a hot water bottle, and a heating pad are "warm."
6. Although the children at this level will not understand that they are making sounds to imitate sounds made in the book, they may be able to imitate the actions and enjoy the resulting sounds. This will help them to understand the relationship between their actions and the consequent sounds.
7. The concrete experience of stepping in the grass, dirt, mud, and water will help these children to integrate the vocabulary. Relate the materials to the story and the pictures in the book.

Symbolic Level

1. All of the previous points from the sensorimotor level and functional level apply to children at the symbolic level as well.
2. Children at this level are better able to analyze how things happen and begin to suggest ways in which experiences like fear can be calmed. Help them to think about times that were good, bad, scary, and so forth. What helped them to feel better? How can they feel better when they are mad? Afraid? Help them to think about what they might do the next time they are mad in the classroom or at home. When actual emotional situations arise in the classroom, remind the children of the discussion, and let them practice the calming techniques, such as breathing deeply, cuddling in the beanbag chair or a blanket, and so forth.
3. Extend these children's verbalization about the touch and smell of different materials and how they compare with other materials. Encourage comparison, description, and classification.
4. At this level, children can make their own tape recordings of the different animals they wish to imitate and can play them back. Have these children discuss how the sounds would be different if the animals felt happy or mad.

5. During the experimentation with sounds, discuss when various voices are appropriate. Ask the children questions to prompt their discussion: In what situations is it alright to shout? When do you need to whisper?

6. Emphasize the development of vocabulary, particularly adjectives and adverbs, with these children. Help them to begin to build a "word bank" of new words they like. Let them start their own notebook of words. You can write down the words they dictate and let them "read" them back to you.

MOTOR AREA

The Motor Area can become a meadow next to the bridge in the Dramatic Play: Theme Area, with obstacles, such as hills, bridges, tunnels, and so forth, that need to be navigated over the next couple of weeks. The specific "obstacles" can be modified from day to day, with the children eventually setting up their own path within the Motor Area. See the Dramatic Play: Theme Area to integrate representational play within this area.

Day 1   Create a scene that is similar to that in the story. Lay out a soft green blanket to represent the meadow. Use a table for a bridge, some blue paper for water under the bridge, and a ramp at one end of the table on an incline for the children to climb down into and up out of the meadow. As the children act out the story, they will need to maneuver up and across the bridge and down into the meadow.

WEEK 1

Day 2   Practice some of the motor skills that occur in the story. These include jumping, climbing, kicking, tramping, using a rope to pull yourself up a steep incline, and rolling down an incline. Discuss how far different animals and things (e.g., trolls, people, goats, frogs) can jump, run, and so forth. Let the children jump, mark their landing with a piece of masking tape with their name on it, and then compare and measure the distances jumped. The activities can be done either before the "billy goats" reach the bridge or after they have crossed and arrived at the meadow.

Day 3   A low balance beam can become the bridge, with a focus on danger and falling. The practice of falling safely is a valuable skill to have, and mastery of it can reduce danger and fear and allow for safer risk taking. Let the children walk on the "bridge," with assistance, if necessary, to enhance the sense of personal support. Place a mat on the floor next to the balance beam, and let the children pretend to fall off the "bridge" and roll on the mats. For those who are ready for it, practicing somersaults, shoulder rolls, and forward rolls is a good next step. Playfully and safely rolling off a pile of mats onto other mats can help with the mastery and reduce the anxiety of falls. This activity may best be done to the side of the actual dramatization of the story, as the focus is quite different. You may want to keep the other "bridge" made from the table and ramp available for other children to use.

Day 4   Make human bridges and tunnels. This activity is best with larger groups and can develop visual-motor control, motor planning, spatial awareness, and balance. As a group, the children practice the straddle position (standing with feet wide apart), bear position (on all fours), bridge position (on hands and knees), and tunnel position (two children holding hands while facing each other). Half of the children could be billy goats and the other half bridges and tunnels. When given a signal, the billy goats practice going over and under the bridges and tunnels. When the billy goats have arrived at the meadow, they switch to being bridges and tunnels. Encourage the children to problem-solve how to make long tunnels or bridges.

Day 5   Make a body obstacle course. Besides tunnels and bridges, a billy goat could go over, under, between, and around bodies that represent a tree, a rock, a log, and a frog. Tape written signs and pictures on the children to indicate what they represent. Besides the billy goat being in an upright position, the billy goat could crawl or walk on all fours through the course. How else could the goats move?

Day 1   Make a more complicated obstacle course. Include the troll, who could be a child, a mannequin, or a stuffed shirt with a paper bag head. This particular obstacle course can use rope woven in, around, and through objects that the billy goats have to follow to avoid being captured by the troll, who by now knows how tricky the billy goats can be. Add road signs, such as "stop," "yield," "one way," "steep hill," and so forth.   **WEEK 2**

Day 2   New challenges can be added to the obstacle course (e.g., ladders, chairs, tables to climb over and under). If you have children in your classroom who use wheelchairs, have different materials on the floor that they can roll over and objects that they have to go around.

Day 3   Add a climbing structure to the obstacle course.

Day 4   Let the billy goats take turns leading other billy goats through the now-familiar obstacle course, using words as well as physical guidance. Some children may want to try going through with their eyes closed or with a blindfold. (Remember, though, that for some children, blindfolds are very uncomfortable and scary.) This peer pairing can emphasize another way friends can make each other feel safe.

Day 5   Let the children spend some time planning changes to the obstacle course by repeating some parts or making some parts easier or harder. They may also choose to change the style by planning to sneak through the obstacle course in absolute silence so that the troll cannot hear them. They might choose to place a small blanket over part of the obstacle course to make it more secretive. They might choose to change the characters of the story so that they are playing other kinds of animals, some of which may need protection from other animals. Encourage creative changes. Have materials ready to stimulate ideas.

After the changes are ready, the children can direct you first and then other children through the altered approach.

Sensorimotor Level

1. Depending on their physical abilities, children at the sensorimotor level may be able to participate in all or part of the obstacle course. Some may need adult facilitation for certain movements. If a child is immobile, he or she can participate by becoming an obstacle in the course or a cheer-leader. Be open to a number of ways to move through parts of the obstacle course (e.g., crouching; crawling; riding in a wagon, on a scooter board, or in a wheelchair). Let all of the children try these different approaches as well.
2. Label objects, actions, and position words, and encourage these children to imitate or approximate the words, sounds, signs, or gestures that you are demonstrating.
3. For children at this level who have physical or sensory challenges, think about modifications that are needed or preparations that can be done before movement is begun to assist them in being more successful in their gross motor efforts. (See Chapter 4, Levels of Learning and Domains of Development, in the *Teacher's Guide* for suggestions relating to children with motor disabilities.)

Functional Level

1. All of the points for children at the sensorimotor level apply to children at the functional level as well.
2. Children at this level who have difficulty with motor planning will need to repeat the activities a number of times to gain mastery. Depending on each child's abilities, use verbal mediation, gesture, and demonstration as facilitation techniques. Reduce the amount of assistance given with each more successful attempt.
3. Give children a reason to move. They should *want* to participate not just participate because they are told to do so. You can incorporate parts of the story into the play. For example, jumping, climbing, or kicking may be used as an attempt to scare the troll or a way to celebrate making it across the bridge.
4. Emphasize the sequence of observing, imitating, and taking turns with these children.
5. These children can also be encouraged to model for others.

Symbolic Level

1. Again, all of the previous points, both from the sensorimotor level and the functional level, apply to children at the symbolic level as well.
2. Children at this level can look at the course and identify the general sequence as it parallels or relates to the story. Encourage these children to act out the story and describe what is happening as they move down the "path" to the bridge.
3. These children can guide a child who is less able or ready through the obstacle course.
4. Omit an obstacle from the course, and see if the children at this level can remember what is missing and replace it.
5. These children can rearrange the course and modify the story. For example, the little billy goat might be frozen in fear and the big billy goat might come to protect him and send him on his way. You can propose "what if" propositions, which are appropriate for this level, and help the children think about alternatives.
6. The children at this level may be more motivated to complete the course "because it is there," but they also need to be motivated to initiate the actions. Emphasize the story and why the billy goats need to get to and across the bridge.
7. With children at this level, you can discuss why a specific object is used as a hill or cave, helping the children to see the similar characteristics.
8. Incorporate discussions with these children about how, when, where, why, and who whenever possible to encourage analytical thinking.
9. Discuss how an object can be both a bridge, for the billy goats, *and* a tunnel, for the troll. Help the children to identify the characteristics of both.

FLOOR PLAY

Day 1 Begin creating a miniature scenario of the story. Tape together green poster board to make a large "grassy" area. This area will be developed over the next 2 weeks. Have the children make a sign for the custodian that reads, "Please do not remove." Have a large bundt pan or other doughnut-shaped gelatin or cake mold available. The children can add water to the pan for a river. Have a variety of types and sizes of small blocks available for the children to build bridges, fences, barns, and so forth. Have puzzles available that include frogs and other outdoor animals for the children to take apart and put together.

Day 2 Continue to play with and add to the miniature scenario. Add plastic animals (including goats, a frog) and a troll doll. The children may want to modify, add to, or remove some of what they made the previous day. Have available puzzles, such as mother and baby puzzles or farm scene puzzles. Play a card game (many versions are available) of Go Fish!

Day 3 Continue to play with and add to the miniature scenario. Add small rocks and nature materials to the scene. Play Baby Animal Lotto.

Day 4 Continue to play with and add to the miniature scenario. Add Tinker Toys to make a bridge. Add small signs for the bridge, meadow, barn, troll, cave, and so forth. Play Baby Animal Lotto.

Day 5 Continue to play with and add to the miniature scenario. Add felt for hills and grass. Let the children choose how they want to modify the scene. Put together a giant puzzle, such as Farm Friends Giant Floor Puzzle.

Day 1 Continue to play with and add to the miniature scenario. Add clay to make rocks. Have available large cardboard and wooden blocks along with a balance beam and various lengths and widths of boards. Suggest that these materials might be used to build a bridge. Experiment with different ways to build a bridge. Talk about "high" and "low," "narrow" and "wide."

Day 2 Continue to play with and add to the miniature scenario. Add a mirror for a pond. Have the blocks and cardboard available again. Add pieces of cardboard of varying lengths and widths. Discuss the "strength" of the various materials. Experiment again with building different bridges and caves with the large blocks and cardboard. Add stuffed animals and dolls to the area to encourage the children to create a story with the materials. Their story will probably have some of the same elements of *The Three Billy Goats Gruff*. You can suggest variations and model different actions with the stuffed animals and dolls to prompt divergent thinking and problem solving.

Day 3   Continue to play with and add to the miniature scenario. Add puppets made at Table Play. Continue the block play, constructing bridges, caves, tunnels, and so forth. Add a cardboard box that the children can use as a cave under their bridge. Suggest alternative story lines. Perhaps the troll or dolls could invite the stuffed animals in for lunch. Repeat Farm Friends Giant Floor Puzzle.

Day 4   Continue to play with and add to the miniature scenario. Add Lincoln Logs to make a bridge.

Day 5   Continue to play with and add to the miniature scenario. Continue the block play with stuffed and plastic toy animals and dolls. Repeat the puzzle play and board games.

Sensorimotor Level

1. Children at this level will not relate the miniature scenario to the story. They will, however, enjoy playing with the animals, water, and toys in the scene. You can encourage the development of representational play by modeling for the children. Have the animals pretend to walk, to eat, and to drink.
2. Encourage children at this level to label the toys and make animal noises and other sounds (e.g., "crash!" when the blocks fall down).
3. These children will particularly enjoy the wind-up or switch toys. Let them experiment with discovering how to make them work before demonstrating.
4. Prompt longer thought sequences by extending the children's actions through modeling. Add a piece of cardboard to the blocks, for example, and then give the child a piece of cardboard, too.
5. With the puzzles and games, label the pictures. Let the children at this level help place or push the pieces onto the board or puzzle.

Functional Level

1. The children at this level will probably use the same one- or two-step sequence of actions repeatedly. Encourage children at this level to remember or create a three- or four-step sequence of actions by modeling new actions and pointing out the actions of their peers. Directing their attention to the actions of others will prompt imitation.

2. Encourage cooperative turn taking in putting the puzzles together, playing the games, and building the structures. You can facilitate this by asking, "Whose turn is it now?"
3. Label the actions and descriptors as you play: "You are building your bridge very tall!"
4. Children at this level will need facilitation to move them from simple construction into dramatic play. Model incorporating the animals and dolls into the miniature scenario and other floor play.
5. Encourage children at this level to examine the pictures in games and puzzles to discriminate differences. On puzzle pieces, help them to see body parts, colors, and shapes that can be matched.

Symbolic Level

1. Children at this level will benefit from the ability to create and expand the miniature scenario. Leaving the materials out over the 2 weeks enables the children to have an ongoing project that grows and changes with each day. Encourage divergent thinking by asking questions, such as "What would be something else we could use for a cave?"
2. Encourage the development, modification, expansion, and elaboration of a story line with the miniature scenario and the block building.
3. Involve the children at this level in making the labels and signs for the miniature scenario.
4. Children at the symbolic level can be leaders in initiating and maintaining a turn-taking sequence. You can facilitate such leadership by your support (e.g., "Jamie, you are doing such a nice job of helping Maya know when it is her turn").
5. Encourage comparison, discrimination, and classification during the play (e.g., "Let's put all of the long blocks over here, so they'll be ready to use on the bridge," "It looks like this puzzle piece has a piece of the foot. Let's see if we can find a piece with the rest of the foot on it").

TABLE PLAY

Day 1

Begin work on creating a puppet stage. (*Note:* this project may take several days to complete.) The puppet stage can be made from a medium-size cardboard box (2' x 2' is about right). Remove any box flaps on the top of the box, and turn the box over on its side so that the top of the box is now the front of the stage. Cut a section (approximately one third to one half of the area of the back) out of what is now the back of the box so that the opening allows the children to place their hands through the back, along the bottom of the stage to operate their puppets. This part can be completed ahead of time, but if time permits, let the children help plan and execute the design of the theater. Involvement in making the puppet stage will inspire the children to want to use it.

Give the children a piece of cloth slightly larger than the front opening of the puppet stage. Lay it out on the table and let the children design a stage curtain using paints, markers, plastic needles and thread, sequins and glue, and so forth. When the stage curtain is completed, attach it across the top of the stage with strong tape or staples so that it can be lifted when a performance is being conducted.

All of the puppets made throughout this module can be used in conjunction with the puppet stage. (When completed, leave the puppet stage out on the top of a table during the entire module, along with containers for the puppets. The children can then dramatize the billy goats gruff story with their puppets and the puppet stage whenever they want.) Set chairs in front of the puppet theater for an audience and chairs behind the box and table for the puppeteers. The children will be able to insert their hands in the opening behind the box to manipulate their puppets.

Day 2

Continue to work on the puppet stage. Make billy goats and troll walking puppets. Supply a picture of a goat and a troll. Let the children choose one of the pictures, color it, cut around it, and then paste it on a piece of cardboard. Using a hole punch, help the children make two holes about ¼" apart at the base of the drawing. (To make them large enough for the children's first two fingers, you will need to punch a hole, then expand it by punching two more holes that overlap the first.) Make each hole large enough to let a finger through. Squeezing the hole punch requires hand strength and coordination. Although they may need assistance, let the children do the punching as independently as possible. Show the children how to put two fingers through the holes to make the legs of the puppet. Let the children use the finger puppets to act out the story. You can encourage children to choose different pictures by making one of each picture for each group of four children who come to the Table Play area. These children can then perform for other children.

Day 3   Continue making the puppet stage. Continue making walking puppets. Let the children paint an inverted shoebox as a bridge. Cut a hole on one side for the troll's cave. They can use items from nature, such as rocks and grass, around the bottom of the bridge. The bridge will stimulate children to have their walking puppets interact in acting out the story. Repeat performances of the puppet show.

Day 4   Create a nature scene for the puppets. Discuss some of the things the billy goats might see as they cross over the bridge to the other side. What are some of the nature objects they might encounter? Show the children items they found outside on the previous day during Outdoor Play. Let the children make a scene for their puppets. Use a piece of cardboard the size of the interior of the puppet stage for the base of the scene. Let the children paint green grass on the inside of the cardboard with a blue river running through it. The river can be painted or made of ribbon, cloth, or corrugated paper. When the paint is dry, let the children tape or glue the shoebox bridge onto the base. They can then use the nature items (e.g., rocks, grass, leaves) gathered outside to decorate the areas around the bridge. When finished, the scene can be put inside the stage and placed on a table along with the puppets. The stage, scene, and puppets can remain out on the table as a play choice for the rest of the module. If the fishing game was not constructed prior to class, the children can make it at this center (see Dramatic Play: Theme Area, Week 1, Day 5 for directions).

Day 5   Make magnetic goats and trolls. Obtain scraps of material that have various furry or rough textures. Let the children cut out pieces of the material and then position and glue the pieces on an oval, circle, or square of cardboard to make a goat. Give them each a small refrigerator magnet (available from hobby shops), and let them glue the magnet onto the back of the cardboard. Let other children use other scraps of material to make a troll. Place a refrigerator magnet on the back of the troll. Place a magnetic board out for the children to use to manipulate their characters. Some children may want to make a bridge from Popsicle sticks with magnets glued to the back or make trees from Popsicle sticks with tree tops made from construction paper attached. Add magnetic letters to the board so that some children can experiment with writing words from the story as well. Have the magnetic board available for the growing number of props and characters. If too many children want to play with the magnetic board or the puppet stage, have a sign-up sheet on which children can write their names (or you can write their names). Continue puppet stage play.

Day 1   Continue puppet stage play. Continue magnetic board play. Create and play the Troll Mouth game. Use the spring type of clothespins to make troll mouths that open and close. You can either leave them as they are or let the children paint white strokes on each side of the "mouth" to represent teeth. Cut several sets of three different sizes of green sponge (to represent the billy goats) for the troll to eat. The children can do this fine motor game alone, in pairs, or in trios. Let each take turns naming what size billy goat he or she is going to eat (e.g., "I'm going to eat the big billy goat!"). The child can then pick up the corresponding size piece of sponge with the clothespin mouth and place it in a container. This game can proceed with turn taking, but children are more likely to turn it into a game of who can eat the most! Either way, the children are having fun and practicing prehension skills.

Day 2   Repeat the Troll Mouth game. Continue puppet stage play. Continue magnetic board play. Using magnetic, plastic, or paper shapes, let the children design trolls, goats, or other animals and characters. Let them tell you about what they made and describe the different parts.

Day 3   Repeat making animals and characters from shapes. Continue puppet stage play. Continue magnetic board play.

Day 4   Continue puppet stage play. Encourage the children to make up new stories. Continue magnetic board play. Make playdough, using a picture chart to illustrate the following recipe:

PLAYDOUGH

1 cup of flour
⅓ cup of salt
1 cup of water
1 tablespoon of vegetable oil

   Let the children measure and mix the ingredients together. Ask them to differentiate between the flour and salt by feeling both with their eyes closed. Ask them to observe what happens when you add liquid. The playdough is ready immediately and will last up to 1 week, if refrigerated. You can also add tempera paint to color the playdough.

Let the children use various tools to make bridges, caves, goats, trolls, grass, and so forth out of the playdough. Add small blocks to make bridges, as well.

Day 5   Continue magnetic board play. Continue play with playdough. Add Tinker Toys and various types of blocks to make bridges and characters to stand in the dough. Continue puppet stage play. Gather together all of the puppets made in the past 2 weeks. The children can act out various scenes from the story with the puppets of their choice on their puppet stage. They can ad-lib as they remember scenes from the story, making up new dialogue. Let the children purchase "tickets" made in the Literacy Center for the performance. You can also use real ticket stubs saved from movie, theater, and sports events.

Sensorimotor Level

1. Children at this level can be involved in the puppetry, both as a part of the audience and as a participant. Though they may not be able to make a puppet (a peer may assist in making puppets for these children), they can use a crayon or marker to make marks on the puppet and can attempt to put their fingers through the holes of the puppet "legs." Encourage them to try to squeeze the hole punch with assistance from you.
2. Children at this level can play with putting materials in and then taking them out of a shoebox. They also may be able to distribute the needed materials: "Missy, I need a rock. Give me a rock, please."
3. Encourage these children to participate in all aspects of making the props and materials, even though they do not relate the materials to the story. The goal for them is to increase their exploration and abilities to manipulate materials and to practice making sounds and words.
4. These children may enjoy attaching letters and figures to the magnetic board. Let them work with a peer, who can take turns putting items up on the board. Encourage the peer to talk to the child and label what he or she is doing.
5. Squeezing the clothespins open is a good activity for these children to increase finger strength and prehension skills. Encourage them to try to pick something up with the tool.
6. Playdough is another good material for children at this level (who are not "mouthers"). Model poking, pushing, squeezing, and so forth.

Functional Level

1. Children at the functional level are able to recognize the pictures of the characters and can begin to do simple dramatic representations. They will need assistance with cutting out the puppets but will be able to assist with the other aspects of making them. Discuss the body parts of each puppet and relate the children's fingers to the legs of the animal to help them understand the representation.
2. Relate all of the puppet play to the story so that the children at this level will have another way of understanding the story sequence and vocabulary.
3. Although these children may need assistance with some of the actions in making the projects, they can benefit from your discussion about the process. Label the actions that they are performing ("coloring"), the characteristics of the materials ("sticky"), and relational words ("under," "through").
4. Encourage the children at this level to pretend the clothespins are mouths opening and closing. This will motivate them to pretend that the clothes-

pins are "eating" the sponges. This is a good activity for increasing the accuracy of their fine motor control, an important component of drawing and writing.

5. Prompt dramatic play with the magnetic board and playdough by modeling actions and adding dialogue to the play.

6. Children at the functional level should be encouraged to relate the pictures on the chart for making playdough to the action sequence of making the dough.

Symbolic Level

1. Children at this level can be engaged in all aspects of Table Play. They can model for and take turns with other children. Encourage them to discuss their actions with their peers.

2. Let these children examine the pictures in the storybook and decide what is needed for their puppet stage. What materials do they need to find?

3. Label the elements of the puppet stage with small signs made or dictated by the children.

4. Use the magnetic letters to create a sign for the puppet stage announcing the performance and the time.

5. Make the Troll Mouth game into a more structured game by adding dice or a spinner so that two or more children can play. Let the children make up the rules of the game.

6. These children may want to make and "sell" the tickets to the performance in the puppet theater. They can determine all of the information that needs to go on the tickets.

7. Encourage children at this level to make up a script for their puppet play.

8. Children at the symbolic level can be encouraged to use a picture chart for making the playdough.

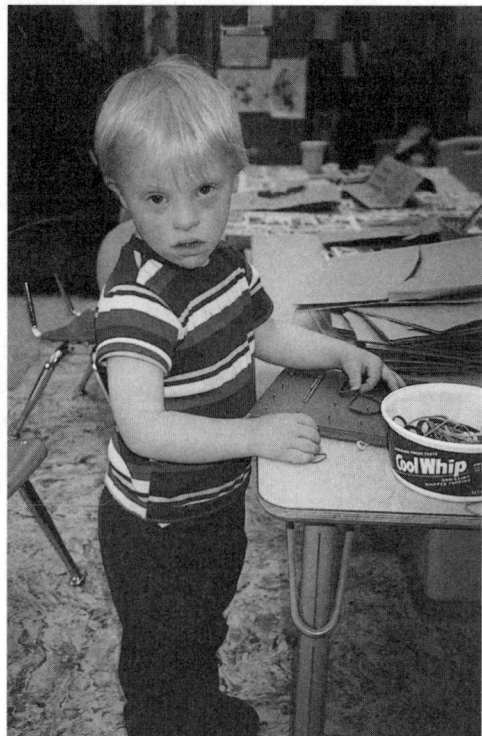

OUTDOOR PLAY

Although a field trip was not included in this module, a half-day trip to a park with a bridge over a small creek would be fun. This would enable the children to role-play the story on a real bridge, play in the grass, and have a picnic. If this is not available, the outdoor activities described next are suggested.

Day 1 Play Troll Hide-and-Seek. This is played like traditional Hide-and-Seek, except a "troll" instead of a person is "it" and must find the hidden "goats." The troll can wear a scary mask and an unusual hat. After the billy goats have hidden, the troll comes to find them. When a billy goat is found, that billy goat becomes the troll. Often children at this age will need some coaching about what it means to be hidden and remain out of sight. Do not worry if some of the children pop out of hiding and announce where they are! Free play.

Day 2 Walk outdoors, and "trip-trap" with loud and soft steps. Place several cardboard boxes around the playground for caves. Play Troll Hide-and-Seek again. Free play.

Day 3 Have a scavenger hunt for objects outside. Make a picture list (with pictures labeled with print) of the objects that are hidden. The objects might be a toy frog, a bridge made of blocks, a troll doll, plastic billy goats, and other outdoor animals. When a child finds an object, he or she brings it back to the teacher, places the object on the picture on the list, and then accompanies a friend who might need help looking for more hidden objects. Free play.

Day 4 Draw a mean troll face on a ball with washable marker. Let the children stand in a circle around the ball. You can start the ball moving by rolling, throwing, head-butting, or kicking it to a child. The point of the game is to keep the ball moving. The children can use any means they want to keep it moving. Free play.

Day 5 Use various outdoor playground equipment to create an outdoor dramatic area to reenact the story. Take the green blanket outside or use a real grassy area to represent the high meadow. Climbing bars and planks or a balance beam can be used to create a bridge. Other items, such as slides, teeter-totters, swings, and riding toys, can become different parts of the path to the high lush meadows. You may want to place numbers on the equipment and suggest that the children follow and play on each item in sequence on their way to the meadow. Have a snack waiting on the blanket or grass.

Make tin-can stilts. Turn two empty soup cans or other similar cans upside down. Using a can opener, make two holes on the bottom of each can opposite each other. Thread both ends of a heavy cord or clothesline through the holes so that the ends can be knotted together inside the can. The cords should be long enough to reach the hand of the child who is standing on the can as he or she pulls up on it for support (approximately a yard long, before being threaded through both sides). The children stand on the cans and hold a rope in each hand. They pull each foot up by pulling on the attached rope. Have the children make "trip-trap" sounds as they walk with the stilts. These stilts are short enough to be safe but high enough to require balance, coordination, and motor planning. Free play.

Day 1   Play Leap Frog in the grass. Show the children how to position their bodies to be crouched down like a frog and how to use their hands on the back of another child to push themselves up and over the child. Many children will undoubtedly need some assistance with this motor planning, but they will have fun trying! In addition to, or instead of, Leap Frog, place large pieces of green construction paper cut into the shape of lily pads on a path through the playground. (You may need to weight them down with stones so that they do not blow away.) The children can then practice jumping like frogs from lily pad to lily pad. Repeat play with the tin-can stilts. Free play.

Day 2   Make a stuffed troll out of old pantyhose and an old shirt. Dress the troll, and hang it from a tree or the swings. Let the children take turns throwing a Nerf or tennis ball at the troll. One child can stand near the troll to retrieve the balls and throw them back. This activity presents a good opportunity to discuss the rules about which objects can be thrown and at what, emphasizing that throwing balls at real people is against the rules and could hurt someone. Free play.

Day 3   Play Troll, May I? Play this game in small groups. Let three of four children stand in a line, side by side, as billy goats. Let another child play the troll and stand with his or her back to the line about 10 feet away. Each of the children takes turns asking permission to take baby steps, middle-size steps, or big steps. Each may ask for up to 10 steps. For instance, "Troll, may I take three baby steps?" The Troll answers, "Yes, you may" or "No, you may not." Each billy goat moves forward as instructed. They can also sneak a step, but if the troll catches them, they have to start over. The first person to reach the troll gets to become the troll, and the troll becomes a billy goat. You will have to assist with this game, but it offers opportunities for understanding size, asking questions, moving in graded steps, and taking turns.

Let the children draw trolls, goats, and bridges with sidewalk chalk. Free play.

Day 4   Make rubbings of various textures found outside. Explain to the children what goats need to eat to grow. Let the children find and place grasses, weeds, and small branches between two pieces of typing or construction paper on the sidewalk. Give each child a piece of sidewalk chalk, and show them how to rub it on its side on the outside of the top piece of paper. As the children color over the top paper, the outlines of the items below will show through. Label each with the name of the child who made it and the items on his or her paper. These can be posted in the classroom or sent home to share with the family. Free play.

Day 5   Make homemade ice cream. This is sometimes a messy activity because of the ice needed, so making it outdoors is a good idea. Goats are good producers of milk, and one of the things they do with grass, trees, shrubs, and weeds is to turn them into good milk. Explain that you are going to use cow's milk instead of goat's milk for the ice cream. Borrow an ice cream maker, and follow the directions for using it. Make a picture chart to accompany the process. Preparing the ingredients, pouring them in, closing up the mixer, and turning the crank all lend to the excitement and anticipation of the ice cream. The process takes some time, so children can play between their turns. Free play.

Sensorimotor Level

1. Children at the sensorimotor level are not yet able to understand games with rules, but they can participate by imitating their peers or being assisted by an adult. When these children are uninterested in an activity, they may be given developmentally appropriate toys and allowed to engage in free play.
2. Movement will often stimulate these children to make noises. Model different sounds (e.g., "whee") for children at this level.
3. Label these children's actions (e.g., "You're swinging," "JUMP! JUMP!").
4. Use action signs for children at this level who do not talk. Teach them signs that they may frequently need (e.g., "MY TURN"; "HELP, PLEASE"; "PLAY WITH ME").
5. Refer to Chapter 4 in the *Teacher's Guide* for adaptations when working with children with motor disabilities.

Functional Level

1. All of the points for children at the sensorimotor level apply to children at the functional level as well.
2. Children at this level do not understand the consistency of rules in the game yet. They can be coached on what actions to take and may remember if it has been modeled several times.

3. Give cues to remind these children of appropriate actions (e.g., "Frogs jjj---"; "Let's count your baby steps: One, two, -----").
4. For games such as Troll, May I? you may need to provide part of the request for these children. For example, after consulting with the child, you might say, "Troll, Megan would like to take one big step." Megan can then be prompted to say "May I?"
5. You may need to give children at this level ideas for where to hide. They will probably emerge quickly.
6. Outdoor activities allow these children to run and get exercise, but you will need to facilitate their participation for them to get the most out of the activities.

Symbolic Level

1. All of the points for children at the sensorimotor level and at the functional level apply to children at the symbolic level as well.
2. At this level, children can reach some agreement about how the game will be played, but they may choose to change the rules frequently. Be tolerant of this behavior, but help them to understand why we have rules that stay the same.
3. Children at this level may also coach others about what to do. They may be paired with other children who need a model.
4. During the activities, continue to use with these children the vocabulary that has been used in the classroom related to the story. The more applications of a word children have heard, the more likely they will be to use the word.
5. Use "What will happen if . . . ?" questions. For example, "What will happen if the troll turns around and sees you sneaking?"

SNACK

Day 1   Oral motor: Show the children how to stick their tongues in and out like frogs. Pretend you are frogs trying to catch flies. Do the Three Frogs fingerplay (see More Suggestions).

Snack: Serve goat salad. Make a salad from different types of lettuce. Show the children each kind of green as you add it to a large bowl. Let each child taste each type. When all the varieties are in the bowl, let several of the children try to use salad tongs or two spoons to mix it up. Add a simple salad dressing. Let the children serve themselves some salad. Discuss which animals eat greens. Pretend you are goats and eat your salad. (You will be surprised how many children who do not eat salad at home will eat their goat salad!) Have carrot juice to drink.

Day 2   Oral motor: Repeat the frog tongue activity. Sing "Are You Listening?" (see More Suggestions).

Snack: Have three different sizes of bread on three different sizes of plates, and ask the children to differentiate among the sizes. Place a "1" by the small cocktail bread slices, a "2" by the plate of French bread slices, and a "3" by the plate of regular bread slices. Have the children tell you, or a "waiter," which slice they would like: one from the "first" plate, the "second" plate, or the "third." Some children may request a "big" or "little" piece. Encourage children who just point to what they want to use a label appropriate to their level (e.g., "bread," "small bread," "second plate"). Let each child choose butter or peanut butter to spread on his or her bread. Serve milk to drink, and pretend it is goat's milk.

Day 3   Oral motor: Pretend to be trolls gnashing teeth. Show your big teeth. Open and close your mouth. Click your teeth. Sing "Are You Listening?"

Snack: Let three different children serve the snack: small, medium, and large carrot sticks; small, medium, and large green pepper sticks; and small, medium, and large celery sticks. Each server can distribute a different vegetable, giving each child one of each size of vegetable. Serve vegetable juice to drink.

Day 4   Oral motor: Do the Three Little Billy Goats fingerplay (see More Suggestions). Experiment with noises that a troll might make when he is happy, sad, or mad. Let the children make up sounds for the others to imitate. Silly noises are acceptable.

Snack: Troll's nose on a bun. Heat frozen appetizer-size sausages wrapped in a roll or croissant in the toaster oven. Call the sausages troll's noses; the children will find this hilarious. Have milk to drink.

Day 5

Oral motor: Repeat troll's faces and noises. Do the Three Little Billy Goats fingerplay.

Snack: Let the children spread a small amount of cream cheese on some crackers. Then give them each a small pile of alfalfa sprouts (like the grass in the meadow) to place on top of the cream cheese. Have water to drink.

Day 1

Oral motor: Do the One Billy Goat fingerplay. Practice making animal hoof sounds. "Trip-trap! Clip-clop!" Use the lips and tongue to experiment with making clicking, popping, and banging noises.

Snack: Have spinach pasta (it's green) with butter mixed in. Sprinkle shredded parmesan on top for hay. Serve milk to drink.

WEEK 2

Day 2

Oral motor: Sing "Ten Little Billy Goats" (see More Suggestions). Pretend to be goats eating grass. Take a big bite, chew it slowly, and say "MMMM."

Snack: Cook green beans so that they are still crisp. Serve them to the children, and let them try to eat them with a spoon, a fork, and their fingers. Have juice to drink.

Day 3

Oral motor: Sing "Old MacDonald Had a Farm." Exaggerate the animal noises.

Snack: Have frogs on a log, which is celery with cheese spread in the crevice and raisins lined up on the cheese spread. Serve water to drink.

Day 4

Oral motor: Repeat songs and actions from previous days. Let children choose.

Snack: Have sliced cucumbers with crumbled feta (or goat) cheese. Discuss how goats give milk like cows and that it can be made into cheese. Have slices or chunks of another type of cheese made from cow's milk to compare. How are they different? Serve juice to drink.

Day 5

Oral motor: Repeat songs and actions from previous days. Let children choose.

Snack: Have goat's horns. Give each child a plate with Bugles crackers and a small amount of cheese dip. Have juice to drink.

Sensorimotor Level

1. Children at this level should be encouraged to imitate the sounds and oral-motor movements during oral-motor play and songs. This will help develop the lip and tongue movements needed for speech.
2. Encourage the children to try the different tastes and textures of the various foods. Some may not like such tastes as goat cheese, but exposure to the tastes will encourage differentiation and help to expand preferences. You may be surprised at some of the flavors the children do like!
3. Even though the children at this level should be given the different sizes of bread, carrots, and so forth, they may not be able to distinguish sizes. They will benefit from looking at differences and hearing the labels.
4. Involve all of the children in discussions about the food and drink. If the children do not have words, read their cues and comment on what they seem to be intending to communicate (e.g., "Samantha is reaching for more cheese. She likes it").

Functional Level

1. All of the above apply.
2. Children at this level may be more successful with comparing two sizes at a time, rather than three. Talk about "big" and "little."
3. Label and describe the food that is being eaten.
4. Discuss the colors, shapes, and so forth.

Symbolic Level

1. Children at this level can help analyze the snack items and discuss the relationship to the story (e.g., spinach, alfalfa).
2. Discuss what items like cheese are made from and how they relate to animals.
3. Let the children at this level lead the songs.
4. Compare the three sizes of items. Use terms such as "big," "bigger," and "biggest."

HOW TO INVOLVE FAMILIES

Families can be involved in the story of *The Three Billy Goats Gruff* in many ways. A week or so before the book is read, send caregivers a letter letting them know what you will be reading. Include with the letter a list of needed items that they may be able to help supply, the vocabulary list from the beginning of the module, and the planning sheets from the beginning of the module. The following is a sample of the first letter:

Date

Dear families,

Next week we will begin reading *The Three Billy Goats Gruff*. This is a fun version of the old tale of the three billy goats who are trying to get across a bridge to the grassy meadow on the other side. A mean old troll is sitting under the bridge threatening to eat the billy goats as they cross over. The billy goats are brave and clever, however, and outsmart the troll.

During the next 2 weeks, we will be exploring the story and talking about how family members support each other, help each other face their fears, and have fun together. We will be doing many activities that explore how we can help each other. You will be receiving a letter from your child requesting that you send in some things to help us. Here is a little forewarning! During the first week, we will be asking you to send in pictures of your family that can be put in a book about things our families like to do together. We will also be talking about things that make us feel better when we are afraid. Your child will be asking you to let him or her bring a stuffed animal or special toy from home. On another day you will be receiving a piece of construction paper with a letter. We would like your family to contribute to drawing or writing on this piece of paper. You may want to trace your hands, draw pictures of each other, or write messages. Your child can then share this family project with the class.

We will also be acting out the story, exploring the things animals eat, making art projects, and doing lots of other fun activities. We welcome you to join us! We have so much fun!

Following is a list of some of the materials we will be needing for our fun at school. If you can help us by donating any of these materials, we would really appreciate it! (Please be sure to label any items that you want returned.)

- Cardboard toilet paper or paper towel tubes
- Clothespins that open and close
- Cotton
- Empty (clean) food cans
- Face paint for the troll
- Green blanket
- Green food coloring
- Heavy or large boots
- Large cardboard boxes
- Loose, large fitting clothing with odd colors for the troll

- Noodles in three different sizes
- Paper plates
- Plastic bottle caps
- Seeds—grass, sunflower, bean, carrot, etc.
- Sponges
- Sunshades and goatee for biggest Billy Goat Gruff
- Toothpicks
- Various weights of jackets to create image of size
- Walking stick for the troll

Thank you!

Sincerely,

Prior to the second week, send another letter home to the family to report on the past week's activities and introduce the coming week. The following is a sample letter:

Date

Dear families,

Thank you for sending in the pictures of your family and your child's favorite things. We have been having fun telling the class about our families and sharing the pictures. We are making books to show you. Goats like to eat grass, and so we are also planting grass seed and watching what happens. We are even going to make "stretchy grass." That should be interesting. Next week we are going to make goat puppets and have a puppet show. You are welcome to come.

    We are still having fun being billy goats and trolls. I make a great troll! We have made bridges to cross over and hide under. We are also making a big mural of the story. You will have to come see all of our great projects!

Sincerely,

MORE SUGGESTIONS

Books

(*Note:* Titles listed below that are preceded by an asterisk are similar to the storybook featured in this module and may be your most appropriate substitutes with modification if you are unable to locate the recommended storybook.)

*Bender, R. (1993). *The three billy goats gruff.* New York: Holt Publishers.

Causley, C. (1986). *"Quack" said the billy goat.* New York: Harper and Row.

*Dewan, T. (1994). *3 billy goat's gruff.* New York: Scholastic.

*Emberley, R. (1995). *Three cool kids.* Boston: Little, Brown.

Fowler, A. (1993). *Woolly sheep and hungry goats.* Chicago: Children's Press.

*Galdone, P. (1996). *Los tres chivitos gruff.* New York: Lectorum Publications.

Hawkes, K. (1991). *Then the troll heard the squeak.* New York: Lothrop, Lee & Shepard Books.

Heller, N. (1990). *A troll story.* New York: Greenwillow Books.

*Liow, J. (1981). *Mice twice.* New York: Athenium.

*McMullen, K. (1995). *Hey, pipsqueak.* New York: HarperCollins.

Milios, R. (1989). *The hungry billy goat.* Chicago: Children's Press.

Morris, A. (1994). *700 kids on Grandpa's farm.* New York: Dutton Children's Books.

Roche, D. (1997). *Brave Georgie goat: Three little stories about growing up.* New York: Crown Publishers.

*Rounds, G. (1993). *The three billy goats gruff.* New York: Holiday House.

Voce, L. (1994). *Over in the meadow.* Cambridge, MA: Candlewick Press.

Wildsmith, B. (1986). *Goat's trail.* New York: Alfred A. Knopf.

Fingerplays, Songs, and Games

ARE YOU LISTENING? (sung to the tune of "Frère Jacques")

Are you listening? Are you listening?
[Hand cupped behind ear.]

Mr. Troll, Mr. Troll.
[Hold a fist to your nose, like a big nose.]

You can hear us coming. You can hear us coming.
[Hand cupped behind ear.]

Trip, trip, trap! Trip, trip, trap!
[Stomp feet.]

ONE BILLY GOAT

One billy goat went out to play,
[Make fingers walk.]

On a wooden bridge one day.
[Walk fingers of one hand cross over the bent other hand.]

He had such a lot of fun,
[Slap knee and laugh.]

He called another goat to come!
[Hands cupped around mouth.]

Two billy goats went out to play . . . etc.
Three billy goats went out to play . . . etc.

TEN LITTLE BILLY GOATS (sung to the tune of "Ten Little Indians")

One little, two little, three little billy goats,
[Start with holding up one finger and add fingers as you sing.]

Four little, five little, six little billy goats,
Seven little, eight little, nine little billy goats,
Ten little billy goats GRUFF!

THREE FROGS

Three little frogs,
[Hold up three fingers of left hand.]

Asleep in the sun.
[Fold them over.]

We'll creep up and wake them.
[Make creeping motion with fingers of right hand.]

Then we will run.
[Hold up three fingers while right hand runs away.]

(Reprinted from "Ring a Ring o' Roses" [p. 119], published by the Flint Public Library, 1026 E. Kearsley Street, Flint, MI 48502 [810] 232-7111.)

THREE LITTLE BILLY GOATS
(sung to the tune of "Three Little Monkeys Jumping on the Bed")

Three little billy goats walking on the bridge,
[Three fingers bounce across the other hand, which is shaped like a bridge.]

"Roar!" said the troll. "Get off my ledge!"
[Put fist under the "bridge."]

Boom! Boom! He kicked one off the bridge,
[Flick one finger of the fist out from under the bridge.]

Just two little billy goats walking on the bridge.
[Two fingers bounce across the other bridge-shaped hand.]

"Roar!" said the troll. "Get off my ledge!"
[Put fist under the "bridge."]

Boom! Boom! He kicked one off the bridge,
[Flick one finger of the fist out from under the bridge.]

Just one little billy goat walking on the bridge
[One finger bounces across the other hand.]

"Roar!" said the troll. "Get off my ledge!"
[Put fist under the "bridge."]

No more billy goats on the bridge.
[Open both hands, palm up.]

Baby Animal Lotto (Otto Maier Verlag Ravensburg, Ravensburger, Germany)

Farm Friends (Otto Maier Verlag Ravensburg, Ravensburger, Germany)

Farm Friends Giant Floor Puzzle (A Frank Schaffer Publication)

Fishin' Fun (Otto Maier Verlag Ravensburg, Ravensburger, Germany)

Frog Game (Pavilion, Geofrey, Inc.)

Hop Along Frogs (Otto Maier Verlag Ravensburg, Ravensburger, Germany)

Rivers, Roads, & Rails (Otto Maier Verlag Ravensburg, Ravensburger, Germany)

Up the River (Otto Maier Verlag Ravensburg, Ravensburger, Germany)

Software   *Art center.* (1993). San Mateo, CA: Creative Wonders.

Bailey's book house. (1993). Redmond, WA: Edmark Corporation.

Facemaker, golden edition. (1986). Fairfield, CT: Queue.

Hallmark connections card studio. (1995). Richardson, TX: Micrografx, Inc.

Sammy's science house. (1994). Edmark, WA: Edmark Corporation.

Talking textwriter. (1986). New York: Scholastic New Media.

WiggleWork® story pack 1. (1986). New York: Scholastic New Media.

WiggleWork® story pack 2. (1986). New York: Scholastic New Media.

NOTES

NOTES

NOTES

ORDER FORM

READ, PLAY, AND LEARN! STORYBOOK ACTIVITIES FOR YOUNG CHILDREN
The Transdisciplinary Play-Based Curriculum from Toni Linder

Please send me the following:

_____ **Teacher's Guide** / Stock # 4005 / $45.00

_____ **Module Collection 1**
Stock # 4013 / $125.00

The Kissing Hand, by Audrey Penn
Somebody and the Three Blairs, by Marilyn Tolhurst
Picking Apples & Pumpkins,
    by Amy and Richard Hutchings
The Little Old Lady Who Was Not Afraid
    of Anything, by Linda Williams
The Knight and the Dragon, by Tomie dePaola
Night Tree, by Eve Bunting
Abiyoyo, by Pete Seeger
The Snowy Day, by Ezra Jack Keats

_____ **Module Collection 2**
Stock # 4021 / $125.00

A Porcupine Named Fluffy, by Helen Lester
The Three Little Javelinas, by Susan Lowell
First Flight, by David McPhail
Franklin Has a Sleepover, by Paulette
    Bourgeois and Brenda Clark
Friends, by Helme Heine
The Rainbow Fish, by Marcus Pfister
The Three Billy Goats Gruff, by Janet Stevens
A Rainbow of Friends, by P.K. Hallinan

ADDITIONAL TRANSDISCIPLINARY PLAY-BASED RESOURCES

Transdisciplinary Play-Based Assessment uses a play-based process with accompanying Observation Guidelines to assess a child's abilities and learning styles. Intervention guidelines in the companion volume, *Transdisciplinary Play-Based Intervention,* help individualize instruction to match each child's developmental level and personal characteristics. Forms to use with TPBA and TPBI are sold separately. Two training videotapes, developed by Toni W. Linder, are also available.

_____ **Transdisciplinary Play-Based Assessment** / Stock # 1626 / $44.00
_____ **Transdisciplinary Play-Based Intervention** / Stock # 1308 / $49.95
_____ Order **TPBA** and **TPBI** as a **set** / Stock # OLIN / $83.95
_____ **Transdisciplinary Play-Based Assessment and Intervention: Child Program Summary Forms**
    Stock # 1634 / $27.00 (pkg. of 5 tablets)
_____ **And You Thought They Were Just Playing** / Stock # 2223 / $175.00 / VHS videotape / 65 min.
_____ **Observing Kassandra** / Stock # 2665 / $169.00 / VHS videotape / 50 min.

_____ Bill my institution (purchase order must be attached)

_____ Payment enclosed (make checks payable to Brookes Publishing Co.)

___ VISA ___ MC ___ AMEX Credit Card #: _____ Exp. date: _____

Signature (needed for all credit card purchases): _____

Daytime telephone: _____

Name: _____

Address: _____

City/State/ZIP: _____

Maryland orders add 5% sales tax.

Photocopy order form and send to: Brookes Publishing Co., P.O. Box 10624, Baltimore, MD 21285-0624

FAX (410) 337-8539; call toll-free (8 A.M.–5 P.M. ET) (800) 638-3775; or order on-line at **www.brookespublishing.com**

Yours to review for 30 days, risk-free. Contact Customer Service for more information on Brookes Publishing's return policy. Prices subject to change without notice. Prices may be higher outside the United States. Source Code: BA18